Collected Verse Plays

By the Same Author

A BRAVERY OF EARTH
READING THE SPIRIT
SONG AND IDEA
POEMS, NEW AND SELECTED
BURR OAKS
SELECTED POEMS
UNDERCLIFF
GREAT PRAISES
COLLECTED POEMS, 1930-1960

With Selden Rodman

WAR AND THE POET
An Anthology

Collected Verse Plays

By

Richard Eberhart

Chapel Hill

THE UNIVERSITY OF NORTH CAROLINA PRESS

To

THE POETS' THEATRE, INC.

Cambridge, Massachusetts

Introduction

Verse drama is more complicated than lyric poetry, which it may contain. It seems also more difficult than prose drama. Is it a matter of emotion? How much emotion has one got? We have all thought of the mystery of Shakespeare, who could not possibly have experienced everything he wrote about. Then how did he do it? The mystery is in the management of one's experience. We feel that if a modern man, like Eliot, writes only a few verse plays which are considered successful, he has done his duty, and we accord him commensurate honor. But to write thirty-odd plays, all informed variously with genius? It is still a mystery. We have heard of the firm, delicate balance of mind, the swiftness of comprehension and communication, the ease of the operations owing to a championing sensitivity and empathy in the Elizabethan intellectual air, the lack of deterrents, the newness and freshness of the theatre. The facts are still phenomenal.

There must be some motive. I have to come down to my own small efforts now. The motives are the same as those for lyric poetry; they come from a basic split in the soul and a need to create, to compensate, to make a whole world. There is a desire for expansion, for a larger canvas. I am afraid I have to say that verse drama with me has been a thrust of the whole man. It is only when I am totally engaged that I have been able laboriously but intensely to pursue it. I am sorry to say this. I recognize it as a limitation. With greater mental discipline, more control of emotion, possibly with less emotion but with more management of it, one ought to be able to work at it without total engagement. I am sorry, my limitations are certainly apparent to me. If only one could write verse drama with the wholly rational mind, like going to work in the morning. This does not happen. One has to wait for months, years maybe, for a motive sufficiently powerful to inflame one. Then one must have the striking chance. And then maybe it will come off. I speak of the tragic feelings, those of Will. Maybe for comic ones, some new Psyche plane, one could go at it willy-nilly.

I first began writing verse drama in a rudimentary fashion with *Triptych* in the mid-thirties. It is little but fantastic talk, practically no action, all poetry. Percy is an airy sprite who calls himself an "air-engine." John is his down-to-earth foil, a man of sense. There is Priscilla, with all the mystery of the feminine, opposed to them both. This was a simple frame on which to hang a dance of ideas. The play is firm enough in texture to have been thought worthy of production in 1955 by Ruth Herschberger, who produced it at the 1020 Art Center in Chicago.

In the late thirties I wrote *Choosing a Monument*, which only appeared in 1953 in *Undercliff* and is a work not included here. This is also a three-way dialogue, between two brothers and a sister. They talk of family matters. Without conscious analogy, I now see that Philip here is a more revolutionary but the same Percy of *Triptych*; that Roger is John again, with some difference; and that May is a more objectified, particularized Priscilla.

I had not got beyond verse dialogue with three characters.

Then the historic moment came in June, 1950. Lyon Phelps came to our house in Cambridge, Massachusetts, wanting to enlist Molly Howe's and my support toward starting a Poets' Theatre. Several interested poets decided to try their hand at the new form and report any progress in the fall.

I went to Yaddo for the first time in August and was so vitalized with new possibilities that I wrote about one hundred pages of verse drama in three weeks. W. C. Williams was in the next studio; his typewriter sounded little arpeggios through the pine trees as he completed *Paterson IV*. There was also an occasional wood thrush which haunted me, our nearest American sound to the English nightingale, which I had been beguiled into the woods near Madingley in England to hear but had never heard.

How to begin?

One develops by slow, painful gropings. I began, naturally enough, with dialogue. I wrote what I called *Preamble I* as a warming-up exercise. This appeared in the fall of 1955 in *discovery* No. 6, entitled there *A Dialogue. An Author and a Poet talk*. There is use of a Faust motif, some attempt to show the dominance of one character by another, some maybe whimsical blood-letting, but nothing much happens, it is mostly ideational talk.

Then I wrote *Preamble II*, a longer piece, densely packed, again with two characters, this time an Author and a Consulting Author. This piece became a clearing-house for what I considered the main problems of the age as I saw and was able to communicate them.

Actually, I conceived these two pieces as somewhat Shavian prologues or preambles to a full action to come. I should mention before going further that I had also written a verse play called *The Apparition*, produced at the first night of the Poets' Theatre, January, 1951, which seems to be complete in itself; though short, it is comic. The Preambles were meant to be strong intellectual fare for a hardy audience which would be willing to listen to verse for three hours or so in a theatre.

The Preambles have not been produced with a play and probably should not be. They were skirting the problem. The problem is action, action and character inextricably welded. Aristotle was right. The plot is most significant, without which poets may only write a shower of ideas in verse.

Then I began on *The Visionary Farms*, which was meant to be a full play with a fool-proof, workable plot and fully drawn characters. By dealing with a set of circumstances in the twenties I avoided a major problem of the dramatist, how to write about deep things without offending living persons from whom the actions were taken, however they may have been covertly altered for artistic purposes.

When I think of the effort of writing *The Visionary Farms*, the explosive release of energy due to a series of events in the real world, I realize how delicately balanced is the possibility of writing verse drama at all. The conditions have to be just right, and over these one has no or little control. The play is a study of evil Will in a man who wishes to imitate his superiors but can only arrive at their states of life by foul means that will ruin them all. It is a tragedy in this sense, but it is a comedy or tragi-comedy in that nobody directly loses his life, although Ransome loses his honor; all but the wife live through it; and the framework of living-room friends continues to comment as Chorus on the action to the end. This framework of persons was conceived as a sophisticated surround and atmosphere to the inner action, which is complete in itself. I use the same persons in several plays, assuming that more than one play can be used in an evening, the framework of chorus-like commentators lending consistency in any combination of works. Yet the crucial problem in verse drama is how to intertwine plot and character. Any framework of Chorus should be an aid.

Subsequently I wrote *Devils and Angels*, which had a formal reading at The Poets' Theatre in January, 1956. I read it on March 12 at The Library of Congress and later at various universities and colleges. This is in line with what I feel is a natural progression to take in these times. It is difficult to entertain and communicate true tragic feelings in these years. The status of man is undergoing rapid change in the world-picture, and the central bases of our former judgments suffer alteration. In so far as our individualism suffers, tragedy is less possible. But there would seem to be an endless possibility to a new Psyche dimension in the creation of comic verse drama.

I conceived *Devils and Angels* to be a type of Comedy, not on a low level of laughter-producing situations but as a presentation from a disinterested motive of the folly of man caught in the inescapable human predicament. One should thus be able to invent endless scenes and evidences of this predicament. Over all should be a love of man while one is exposing his manifest weaknesses. We can bring the gods in in the form of a devil and an angel on the stage and make up plausible actions. I call the play a Psyche one in that it mainly exists on a plane above Will in its final implications; man may be shown as willful and blind in the interim actions; and there is room for fantasy and byplay, for odd juxtapositions, unusual, perhaps hilarious situations. The Comic drama may have impressionism as a base, which may also be its limitation, but I do not see why it may not be pleasing and instructive and yet stay on a high level of disinterested engagement of the human spectacle.

Now, as with a piece of music, let me play on these

two chords again, the tragic and comic.

Speaking of *The Visionary Farms*, the tragic character is Hurricane Ransome, but he is given two early scenes of somewhat riotous comedy, before his soliloquy wherein he recognizes his duplicity.

Actually, both Parker and Fahnstock are tragic characters, but of circumstances rather than of inner flaws. They neither of them considered that their trusted employer and comptroller was undoing them behind their backs. The play is set in the 1920's, when the upsurge of business growth and success was so great that the president and vice-president, respectively, could not see the illogic of Ransome's huge expenditures on his fantastic chicken farms. All those men are tarred with the same brush; the owners also have extra-business farms and enterprises. It is the son of the president who discovers the flaw in Ransome's company accounts and unmasks him. Perhaps the traditional flaw in the owners is their natural societal blindness, but I consider this as a flaw of circumstance rather than of character. Ransome believes in the baubles of the world so much that he is willing, owing to his weakness, to embezzle in a grandiose, clever way to keep up with the Joneses. He is a have-not who wants to have more. They all have compulsive wills toward big success.

There is a scene in the Apple Orchard in which Fahnstock, the strong father, has to tell his children that his wife is dying of cancer just as he has lost his fortune because of the duplicity of Ransome. We wondered whether this scene, of what would in an earlier century have been known as true emotion, would work as theater, whether it would fail as being sentimental. It must be said that it worked as effective emotion when played by sensitive actors. But the whole piece, while it is an effort toward true tragedy, seems to me to be more nearly a tragi-comedy. The last scene, showing Ransome's prison life after his conviction, tends to bear this out. This last scene was called for by the splendid young group at Seattle who put on the play under the direction of Glenn Hughes. They became so enamored of Ransome that they wanted to know what would happen to him later. This scene was composed for the Seattle production and has been retained since. The first production was at the Fogg Art Museum in 1951; the second at the University of Washington, Seattle, in 1953. The third production was that of the Institute of Contemporary Arts, Washington, D. C., a reading performance at the Corcoran Art Gallery in 1956 in which I was invited to burst upon the scene as author when the author appears. The fourth production was a three-day run at the University of Cincinnati in 1961, with a thoroughly sophisticated and able group which understood and conveyed the meanings and connotations of the play in a most rewarding presentation.*

The play shows the effects of Will, the will power in the main characters to get what they want, and it shows the outcome of dramatic involvement in willful situations.

I have spoken above of the difficulty in these times of entertaining true feelings, true tragic emotions, owing to our lack of belief in and respect for human character.

Devils and Angels moves to the realm of Comedy, or Psyche in a new dimension of it, in the sense that nothing

* The cast: Robin Everyman, Kent Guthrie; Beryl Everyman, Marlana Groen; Jason Curley, Stanley Kravitz; Wendy Curley, Mary Grace Matz; Charlie Westgate, Dick Von Hoene; Grayce Westgate, Betsy O'Neill; Consulting Author, Tom Behrens; Hurricane Ransome, Marvin Vawter; Adam Fahnstock, John Hess; Vine Fahnstock, Eleanor Hazelton; Suzanne Fahnstock, Margaret Tydings; William Fahnstock, Gerard Malanga; Peter Fahnstock, Lee Reams; Mr. Parker, David Murray; Taft, Bill Akin; Bub Woodward, Ronald Ruhl; Frieda Woodward, Barbara Lerner.

Casts of first productions of this and other plays will be found at the end of the book.

is expected to be done about situations, but these are shown as spectacles of human frailty and error. The audience can be disinterested while enjoying the penetration of a devil and an angel into human affairs. If we can laugh at the situation, perhaps we can do so without derision and with a balanced, disinterested sympathy with the human condition. It seems to me at the present time that this is a more suitable type of attitude to take— that is, the writing of Comedy wherein Psyche reigns as an upholder of truth against the faulty Will of man— than if we thought we could write tragedy.

The Mad Musician has the framework of the same characters as in others of my plays. Some parts of the soliloquies go back as poems to the late thirties. The problem of the play appeared gradually. Unlike some of the other plays, which were written in a heat of composition over a short period of time, this was yoked together during the mid-fifties. Both *Devils and Angels* and *The Mad Musician* appear here in book form for the first time.

RICHARD EBERHART
1962

Contents

Triptych

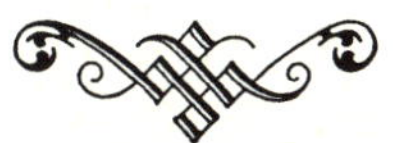

Triptych

PERCY

> Whimsicality is a thing in itself.
> Cast out your noble argument.
> You've only got to go look
> At a child fetched forth from the womb,
> Or see an old codger croak,
> To assume the world is nothing but sorrow.

JOHN

> But, you forget, sir,
> The importance of values,
> Of rigorous discernment among them.

PERCY

> Ha, your cheeks will be long
> Enough to make sizable culverts
> In them, down which to flush
> The tearful sorrows of your seriousness.
> Come, praise whimsicality.
> He's a painted clown can walk a
> Tight rope narrowly, and will fool the people.
> He's your only modern who can't be criticized.
> He's understudy to the true bigwigs,
> Those who experience experience.
> Mark his moony jaws and craven
> Pate, his withal constancy.
> Critics be brought to the tent.
> They have not learnt all.
> They want juice.

JOHN

> My dear sir,
> You run on like an adolescent litterateur.
> Come out of it.
> Let us get down to reality—

PERCY

Ho, reality is up. What's up? So
We are up to reality. I
Insist on levity. There's a
Certain deviltry in all levity.
Let your philosophical discourse
Wait on the slow decay of paper.
The shelves will last and the books on them,
Till the digger worms set up a Piccadilly
And haul stuffs hard through the tubes
That the forage of nature's
Dumped atop the sheaves of art.
Spirit won't keep.
But like the laughter in the throat
It shocks out over the teeth
In a stony springing brook;
Falls over an edge and
Becomes an airy gauze;
Becomes great laughing-crystals.
The worms have no guts,
And must eat only wood and paper.
I am Air-eater,
The hardest, rarest occupation.

JOHN

It is time I praised my own tolerance,
But I have known you so long
I will allow you the pleasures of expansion.
However, I have for the past fortnight
Examined the five volumes of the late Dr. Fardel,
The latinist we knew at the University—

PERCY

If you
Would put all the great brains of
Oxford and Cambridge in a tub
And boil them for three and thirty minutes,
You might beget an elf.

JOHN

As I was saying, the learned Doctor—

PERCY

Oh—I feel a pun coming.
Hmmm. A gross pun, although
All men hate them, is worth more than
A quire of your syllogistic Doctors.

Is an integer of sense, a compound
Of fertility; albeit an indigestible squib.

JOHN

Spare me your puns anyway.
Now, his theory in general is—

PERCY

I wonder if he theorized in his lady's bed.
No doubt, being a Latin scholar,
He went over old conjugations.

JOHN

This so-called merriment of yours
Is merely dull superstructure
You erect upon your ignorance.

PERCY

If I'm ignorant, then I love ignorance.
I'll squeeze it into a voluptuous guffaw then.
And I'll shout ignorance at you
Until you get some sense.

JOHN

Such a belligerent attitude is hardly
Becoming to one of your formal education.
But in our last discussion, I recall
We had seriously got to the point of—

PERCY

The point of merriment at you, sir!
When a man is out of work,
And loitering in his father's plush arm-chair,
It's grand to stalk the realistic pessimists.
But I am for the point of ignition:
Let the intellectual hayricks
In the wet season be burnt up by
The sun's hilarious eye.
Asthma has got a grip on existence.
That is my particular gripe. A jape.
In truth, I am so full of glee I am
More ridiculous than before I said so.
Come, now, have you ever seen
A critic jump a fence?
'Twould be damned bad for his criticism.
I'll bet the barbed wire would
Criticize his backside, make him
Bleed out his petty principles;
He should have jumped higher, and got over the Greeks.

JOHN

> Well, I guess I must leave you
> And go back to my discourses.
> You seem incapable of
> Even an attempt at lucidity.

PERCY

> What, lucidity?
> When Lucy is lucid to me
> I will tempt her and attempt her
> And run and tell thee.
> Pardon, I retch. It must be the acidity.

JOHN

> You make me sick.

PERCY

> Be merry. As long as you are not married,
> You might as well be merry.
> Really, tomorrow I will cry all day.
> I will buy little squirt guns filled
> With sugar water and run them down
> The two lobes of my face,
> To let you know I am crying.
> Tomorrow I will be the soul of solemnity.
> I will go to the Museum and lie down
> Full length in a Medieval stone coffin.
> I did it once, and was so grievous a sight,
> The attendant broke out laughing.
> Let me groan from six o'clock in the morning.
> By noon I will have got the habit,
> And by night I shall be an absolute wailing ghost.

JOHN

> Come, you are not reasonable.

PERCY

> Reason and treason are the same thing to me.
> Reason is too credulous.
> It irks me like old ladies;
> Or old gubernatorial gentlemen.
> Ha! I fly by Absolute Force.
> I am so light the air is my very being
> And I would be all over the sky.
> Your reasoners only poke about in old clothes.

JOHN

> You simply rave against what you love.

PERCY

> If I rave against what I love,
> You fail me in reciprocal
> Love of what you hate.
> Oh, there comes a she.
> Now I must fly against
> The earthly quality of women.
> Hello, vegetable, how's your green hue?

PRISCILLA

> What sport is this?

JOHN

> Good afternoon, dear. My greetings. Don't bother
> About him; he's in a ripe inconsequence,
> And won't bother us a bit. What a lovely frock—

PRISCILLA

> I have just come from town with a car
> Full of sheer things, the smartest things from Paris.
> And these matching jewels from India.

PERCY

> Oh, for a new attitude to death.
> The Polynesians did well when they
> Packed and squeezed the head down to
> The round and look of a sick lemon
> Left over long in the sun. Found embalmers.
> The bulging fellow got down at last,
> Brains confessed in a boy's handful.

PRISCILLA

> What an awful fool. How should I
> Provoke such language, and with my new ensemble?

JOHN

> As host, I must ameliorate
> Between your displeasure and his candour.

PERCY

> I propose tombstones and mausoleums
> Be laid under the pile-driver
> And done into powder for the cheeks of virgins.
> Such quantities of the stuff would be,
> And so few authoritative patronizers,
> They'd be chalked to the death withal,
> Tricked out with the most emaciated spells
> To get their man. Now, these dead.
> What to do with the dead. I once saw a
> Groundhog stick his fat corpse

Into the very light of July.
It blistered, broke loose, and you've never seen
So merry a sight. Soon he was aswim
In his own oils, hot as a lecher,
And then he was dancing with maggots.
In a fortnight he was itching with
A most greedy dissipation,
As hilarious as a bunch of bees,
And strong enough to drive off a troop of buzzards.
By August middle he had got strained
Into a nervous maniacal gymnastic,
And by December his divine frenzy
Was quits with the world.
I passed by the place the next summer,
It had a lonely look.
Indeed, he had only a little hairy ghost.
But it would boil again; and manure the wild flowers.
Now take corpses, stretch them out
In bold capable nakedness
On the ground and see them do likewise.
And liveliness to them!
What a purgative performance.
'Twould make people Buddhistic,
And do away with the wars.
You'd have a better opinion of life
For the stench. Nothing like strong youth,
Strong love, strong corpses boiling,
Quick with effervescence.
And hang on their heaving breasts
The jewels of women. They'll sink
Down slowly in the fleshly mess,
And at the last shine on and dazzle the earth.
An acute eye will pluck the glory
Of their indestructibility.
Page Hieronymus Bosch.

JOHN

You betray yourself, fellow,
And in the name of frivolity
Entertain us with a quite serious notion.
I glimpse even a spiritual
Regenerative principle
In your suggested and unlikely tactic.
But you employ a symbol for your

Metaphysics; otherwise they would vanish.
They would go back to the blood
And become the simple energy of action.
There is no necessity to change
The various burial rites of the world;
They are forms of human decency.
You would do better to apply your fancy
To the living,
Who stand in need of vitalizing notions.

PERCY

Have at you. I am Air-engine.
And incandescence is the sole sweet of the world.

JOHN

You are in danger of becoming a theologian.
If you would put your views
Into a somewhat less heretical mould,
Even encase them in a cloak
Foreign to their character,
You might get a Rockefeller fellowship,
And study a year at Rio.
But you are only man after all,
The actor-animal.

PRISCILLA

Well, apparently I am here
Only as an objective symbol of
Your opinion of women:
I must suffer your talk.
You are always dissatisfied;
Fomenting ideas
As if the world could be changed.

PERCY

There's no more happiness in the world
Than a squirrel has with a nut.
You crack it open, eat it up,
And want more. But ideas
Are everywhere in the sky.
Come, fly by whimsicality.

JOHN

You ought to work for the City Company.
You could wear spikes,
Climb up poles like your ancestors,
And thereby carry electricity to the people.
If you were less ubiquitous and more single

I would want to cope with you.
Come, let me put some salt on your tail.
Your shallowness——

PERCY

Shallow? Then air is shallow,
Through which we see to heaven.
Shallow? Then water is shallow,
Of which we are all composed.
Shallow? Then morning's atmosphere,
Lakes, rivers, rills and streams
Are shallow. What is your jealous depth
But layers and layers of shallows? What
Profundity, but a schoolmaster's
Multiplications of a feather falling.
Shallow? Then I'll lie down on the wee
Boat of a feather, and sail in the heavenly air.
I count on the docility
Of men to save them much trouble.
Here is an old one, a seller of papers,
Bearing his load of defunct news
Homeward in the centre of night.
Life makes him
Faithful to his duty. He says
Good-night gently, when you pass.
And I daresay he is as good as
Your schizophrenic synthetic dictators.
Shallow? Come praise whimsicality.

PRISCILLA

I say, do you mind, I must be leaving——

JOHN

Why, I'm awfully sorry, won't you——

PRISCILLA

Good-bye——

JOHN

You've driven the lovely creature off
With your frail bombast.

PERCY

I must go. This is not what I was.
This is something else. This is pure Phoenix.
Come feel it. No, you can't. For though
You were vampire and drank my blood,
You would not get me. Fetch me
The past in a basket lined with grass,

If you think to. Bring me
A bucket full of huckleberries
Plucked at ten years old, if you will.
Present me my first virgin,
If you can. Or dig up my bones
When I shall have been a decade dead,
If you are able. No, no,
I am something else than I am.
I am the tickings of clocks whose ratchets
Wear away now in the mill stream.
And the rust of them, standing in old barns.
I am the bud of the leaf
Whose remains stick on my heels . . .
Oh, I am the lad's eyes,
When there was wonder upon them
Like flax twinkling in the wind and sun . . .
The same skull; Plato and Aristole,
Plus Shakespeare, and Donne, and Blake, and Marx,
And as gone as old Neanderthal.

JOHN

Would you mind coming along?

PERCY

Oh, that's all right, but the world's
Nothing but a pile of filth. The
Relations between men are as excellent as hell,
They are all well ordered and arranged beforehand.
There's nothing so full of end-results
As friendship; and nothing so crafty
As men in love with mountains.
When you have gone through all,
Evil stares you in the strict, emaciated face.
But you're not emancipated yet.
You can no more conquer yourself
Than walk on Pluto. The good falls
Into a big disrespect and a dusty bin;
Evil flowers out incandescent,
Ready to burn you up again.
The masters of life have as much
Energy as it; the rest fade off.

JOHN

I say, do you mind coming along?

PERCY

There are those who say flowers

Have no more to say; look there,
There is the world pure and final,
Nothing else to it. There are those
Who say those are partial fellows,
Befriended by lenses. These are troubled
By a fire in the guts and say
Microscopes do no good.
The messy little bluet is only
A sallying forth of some knotted ganglia.
They have a great room between the ears,
Wherein they play games. There are others,
Who can hardly tell whether they are
In Venice or Canton, but they are
Sure neither has the importance of a thumb tack.
They doubt they doubt their own doubts,
And end where they began—a right
Doleful dingle-dangle state indeed.
The experimenters are, sooth-la,
The only realizers. That is
Because they refuse to think.
They put chemicals in test tubes,
Measure the results, and have no
Astonishment whatever at the conflagration.
But the artist saves the world.
I have been everywhere, done everything.
There is nothing left but
To search out the bosom of God,
The chief receding pleasure known to man.
The searching is ever better
Than the finding; when you have found something
You must keep it, which is another kind of searching.
If you search for an unknown woman,
You must always be seeking. If you
Marry one, you must, though you have her by you,
Seek out new ways continually to appease her.
Get a child, and you go back to God.

JOHN

Well, come along now, Percy.

PERCY

I have come to no conclusion.

JOHN

You have come to no conclusion.

PERCY-JOHN

> We have come to no conclusion.

PERCY

> Conclusion is too inclusive.
> To(o) crude warfare my food is air.

(Curtain)

Preamble I

Preamble I

House of the Author: The Living Room.

POET

I want to be a world-protagonist.
There is still something to be exaggerated.
There are subterrene mines of Monadnock years
Which need elevation; the ore, got by memory,
Should shine forth a resolute brightness
And restore to man his pleasing directness.
He is locked in indirections locked in fellows;
His close bight, and lack of social reach,
As he is gnashed in cities, accused by legalities,
Flindered in money machines, shucking nervosities,
Make elevation of the mind to him suspect,
And poetry a joust to be laughed at.

AUTHOR

You flay around with the arms of a windmill.
Not a good image. You should be the creator.
I should take you in hand and give you a cause.
To wait on the wind, and be activated by it,
Is, if happily to sing on some Gaspean headland
With a forty-mile sluice of the bright stuff coming,
Only to be played upon by chance. Not good.
I do not talk here about the quality of song.

POET

I feel that I am engine kept in low gear.

AUTHOR

Probably safer, but you need your true nature
Which is to be fast, supple, cunning, a racer.

POET

My struggle is against time and society,
Not against my individualistic nature.
Time is always accreting exciting experience
Which is bogged down in the meshes of man's living.

Partaking of that, as I must, I confess
I struggle against the hardness of the predicament
And spend years of my credulous sensibility
As it were swimming against the stream.
If you have to swim to keep your head
Out of water, how are you to contemplate your navel?

AUTHOR

You have contemplated your navel quite roundly;
I note it as a favorite of your pastimes.
The question is beyond that: it is about society.

POET

Do you really think I am too selfish?

AUTHOR

You are egotistical, egoistical, egocentrical
And so whelmed, sated, and stuffed in self
That society inclines to view you the fool.

POET

Society is always wrong and I am always right.
How does it comprehend Job, or Oedipus,
Except through me? I search the very darkness
And bring up whatever of the very brightness.

AUTHOR

You are, unfortunately perhaps, society's nerve ends,
To shock its consciousness with worlds of that.
Do you get my drift?

POET

                              I assume responsibility,
But the age makes me a thrasher of arms,
One who strikes out wildly in the dark,
With a somewhat preposterous largeness of motions
Which, I admit, I view sometimes as comical.

AUTHOR

Perhaps you have reached a lucky dimension.
I used to engender you to espouse the tragic
(You were fairly young then and had more emotions,
And those more enormously poised and expended
Than the objective situations warranted)
But now I would invite you to approach the comic.
You can be mature, laugh at your fellows,
Take yourself lightly because most serious,
And dance upon the daft concerns of mankind.

POET

I would agree to canalization.

AUTHOR

    Make it new, be spare, keep it fresh.

POET

    Maybe one is blessed by psychological blocks.
    It is the dam on the millstream not only
    Backs up water to make the lily ponds
    And gives the spring peepers joyous concatenations,
    But makes for a swift plunge over the lip:
    Say, there is lucid and some singing water there.

AUTHOR

    You have a point and are talking about freedom.
    Yet, if you were "really free" you would not
    Be really free, but would undoubtedly stagnate,
    Held in a rank wallow, a large misuse,
    And be lost to any flute-like rarity.

POET

    I suppose that eventually I have to submit.

AUTHOR

    I am your author and will do as I see fit.

POET

    What do you want me to talk about, to effect?

AUTHOR

    I would like you to be the poet of the relative.

POET

    All my life I have searched for the absolute.

AUTHOR

    I want you to find the absolute in the relative.

POET

    Natural to me are vague generalities.

AUTHOR

    Be specific, and thus engage totalities.

POET

    I always knew there would be some dreadful
    Loss of my personality. You want me to renounce
    The very godhead of my deep delight,
    My savage selfhood and my fierce esteem,
    My golden auras and my psychic spleen,
    My adamantine and intolerable presages
    And all my lofty insolence and fire,
    My hard-earned insights, my given glimpses
    Graven on marble mind in golden gleams;
    You want me not to be my inviolable self

And lose those night-deep divisions of the mind
And those white flashes of the single flesh,
Profundities of instability
That open up the world in magic fictions
And make me know the truth, and know myself.

(*Distractedly, as if talking to himself*)

I have seen Death himself, in his white robe,
The king of shadows of a painless world,
Walk in the gardens of the evening
Spreading a dream of rose and amethyst
Beyond our knowledge. His face was pure, and white.
Kingly he was, the master of us all,
And as he walked, I fancied our vexed flesh,
Troublesome minds, and trials of pain and sin,
Were purged; I felt our life as little;
I sensed our time a dream whithin a dream.
One day in his still kingdom we would be
Ourselves the dream, walking in silent shadows
In a kind of sweetness, a kind of lightness.
And I have seen Love, the equal partner
Of the world, unmoving, a Madonna of the Rocks,
In the full flesh of breasts and hips,
The principle of nurture and of solace,
Mother who gives the gift of birth,
Who lavishes her ritual of the earth,
Look from shored eyes; her look was full and long,
Beyond her two young, jostling nurslings.
She was a principle of richness, lushness,
Within her gaze and strength all deviate ways
That make up love. Care and action
Were her provenience; her force was universal;
And mostly as I looked she represented purpose.

AUTHOR

Better not carry on too long that way.
I have heard this sort of thing before.

POET

I am restive against your toothy barbs.
You are actually a master of the sinister,
A destroyer, a trap and house of machinations.
You wish me to enter a dark confine.

AUTHOR

You still have the freedom of your will

And need not come with me. You can stay
In the airy fashion of your tentativeness,
But if you wish me to be your architect
You must sit still and listen to my plans.

POET

I must confess you captivate and fascinate,
For I had never any plan: only to be free,
An airy spirit flying gauzy ways,
Fending off the harsh realities of life.
Illusion has been my leader; evasive action
My method; aloofness my impenetrability;
Intellectual clarity my presupposition.
I admit I never came to grips with life,
Living apart from mankind in the spirit,
While most desiring to perform it service.
I thought I served man by my insight dreams,
Clawing my way through scums of melancholy,
Hiding in the tangled woods of introspection.

AUTHOR (*aside*)

You came to grips better than you knew.
Instinct told you what was valuable,
Intuition kept you malleable. (*Aloud*)
How did you evade the realities, as you say?

POET

By teaching the young, of course. I taught them
More than they knew, but less than I wanted to know.
There is nothing so presumptuous as to teach the young.

AUTHOR

Given their condition, somebody has to teach them.

POET

No doubt their instructors altered their lives. Mine
Did mine.

AUTHOR

                                Were you in danger of being subversive?

POET

Subversion one year may be conversion the next.

AUTHOR

I take it you make fun of politics?

POET

                                                        Rather,
Politics makes fun of mortals. The truth
Is no respecter of political parties, right, left,
Front, center.

AUTHOR

                        Would you uphold the Constitution?

POET

        By birthright. Its greatness is its fluidity.
        Each panel of nine old men keeps it mobile.
        We justified our mistreatment of the Indians.
        When I was young it was made to fit socialism.
        It can be make to fit a laboristic society.
        I suppose it could be adjusted to cannibalism.

AUTHOR

        Do you have any political affiliations?

POET

        I thought I had been superior to politics.
        Have you not been listening to my affirmations?
        I see that your purpose is to drag me down.

AUTHOR

        The times will not tolerate a poet
        Who is too far left or too far right.

POET

        What if he is too much in the center?

AUTHOR

        How cynical of you. You must take a stand.

POET

        What if I stand on the top of my head?

AUTHOR

        Come down to earth and stand on your feet.

POET

        Can I get out of this, or do I have to
        Give in for keeps?

AUTHOR

                                The compact is final.

POET

        The unpurged images of day are receding.

AUTHOR

        You have been wandering around while talking.
        Come over here and sit in this chair.
        I want you to seal a compact with me.
        Take this penknife and slit your wrist.
        Here is an eye-dropper. Take out some blood
        And I will put it in this Parker 51.
        On the table there is some paper. With this pen
        Write that you will renounce your individuality

And will henceforth completely do my bidding.
I have in my pocket some band-aids for later.

POET

This is ridiculous, as it is mischievous.
What do you think I am? You are living in the past.
Pen-service to a monstrous archaism!
I'll do nothing of the kind. You, old mole,
Are out of date. I live in the future,
That is, a futuristic present,
Not depending on old literatures for method.
Neither do I lift other poets' lines
To import into and fit among mine.
What do I get out of this?

AUTHOR

                                     How, do you
Rhyme too?

POET

           Sometimes, in rainy weather.

AUTHOR

Come to me. I will give you fame.
You have admitted all along that you are inchoate,
Unconcentrated, flying off every which way,
And that you have no central theme or themes.
By my agency you will become famous.
We both recognize the violence of the ego.
You cannot do it yourself. Come with me
And I will make you famous. Renounce,
Give up, abnegate, discipline yourself.
And furthermore, I will give you women.

POET

Thoroughly out of date! How unintelligent!
I can get plenty of women myself, thank you.
The idea of Pandarus may be Greek
But it is foolish now, and much too simple.
You can go to the Devil.

AUTHOR

                                   Don't you see
That I am the Devil? That is, a sort of Devil.
But we do not believe in him any more,
Which is why you do not thoroughly trust me,
And shy off in your boyish recalcitrance.
My ancient, hypnotic powers of casting spells
Have grown rusty through the centuries.

The modern mind is quite dichotomous.
And so I am also, in a sense, an Angel.
I'll weight it on the angelic side, then.
I'll be your good Angel, if you'll allow the term,
As I am bent and determined to do you good.
(*Aside*)
But who, if I cried, would hear me among the angelic orders?

POET

None of that flesh-cutting nonsense. As I
Am a man of integrity and function integrally
We can dispense with your learned butchery.
By Heaven, here is an example of Progress.
I will of my own free will give in to you,
I will follow you, and let you be
My guide, to become your world-protagonist.
(*Aside*)
I hope it doesn't degenerate into the picayune.

AUTHOR (*faking a Sign of the Cross over the Poet*)
Hence renounce all your princely estates and titles,
Lands contiguous to evanescence, royalties of possession,
Airy nonsense, unprofitable purgations
Linguistical, ambiguous and semantical,
Wishful thinking, individualistic fripperies
Egotistical, egoistical, strategical.
Henceforth, Poet, you are Everyman.

(*Curtain*)

Preamble II

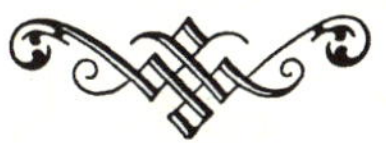

Preamble II

Author and Consulting Author

AUTHOR

    So, you have been keeping close to the nest?

C. A.

    Yes, planning to secrete an egg in the Library.
    A safe mansion, a hundred thousand books.
    I have a vair and vernal feeling there, but
    After the turning and matting of some seasons.

AUTHOR

    Our University thrush!

C. A.

                         Maybe a snake
    In the bushes would gobble the birdies up.

AUTHOR

    Criticism this time?

C. A.

                   Weaving the weather,
    Confecting some niceties of adjudication.
    Song was ever a sifter. Vocalism is to you.
    I am writing a treatise on Dandyism.

AUTHOR

    A nice opposite to your constitutional sobriety.
    I should think it an unmannerly affection;
    Pleasant, no doubt, to be a taster of style.

C. A.

    There was some difficulty with the authorities
    Due to the subject. Puritanism is still warm.

AUTHOR

    Warn it off. Is not scholarship disinterested?

C. A.

    I convinced them of the value of the study
    Due to its lack of relationship with life

As we know it. Its lack of importance
Became a glass through which they saw darkly.

AUTHOR

There is no doubt great wisdom in darkness.
Who, though, wants to have great wisdom? For what?

C. A.

I'll make a kaleidoscope of canny lights,
Perhaps confect some rationale, define symptoms.

AUTHOR

Defunctive music.

C. A.

                    Those birds are still immortal.

AUTHOR

It was good of you to come over. I suspect
It is due to weakness that I asked you.
I would like to consult with you, seriously.

C. A.

Lead on. Don't let seriousness be slavish.
Time makes us wise, obliquely by nuance.
I doubt if I will be able to help you.
What do you have in mind?

AUTHOR

                                    Vast schemes.
I want to write a play with Everyman
Its subject, a gigantic work of force and depth,
Evoking the tragic majesty of mankind,
His flaw laid bare, acquainting his forced rebuffs
With violent images that shock the mind,
Exacerbate the senses from vile lassitude
And hint at some old, lost nobility.
Worlds of meaning are at our fingertips
Could we but catch and clutch them to us.
You know how many years in a kind of writhing
I have seen glimpses of man's greatness,
But ever the age has quashed and cured them.

C. A.

Do not bite off more than you can chew.
You were born out of time, the latest Elizabethan,
And should tack your potential to the useful.
Did you learn anything from the war?

Author

                                    Too much,
And too little. The First is now thoroughly dream.
What's coming keeps us in continuous affright.

C. A.

Our times are too confused for tragic utterance.
Define somewhat narrow limits, I should say,
The age may yet advance to Comedy.

Author

Yes, I see that. Tragedy implies belief;
Comedy, a round view of a spectacle.
We have lost any central doctrine of beliefs,
But we have not stashed our senses yet.
(The telephone rings)
Pardon me.
(Going to phone)
            No, no word yet. I sent them
Two weeks ago. Perhaps he is stultified
At term-end. It may take a while longer.
You can't wait for the verdict? May he give you
A verediction. Maybe you are too difficult;
A revolution may act like a sludge hammer.
Your inspissations may crispen, stiffen to dry.
Good bye.

C. A. *(Offering a cigarette)*

                        Try one of these?

Author

                                Thanks.
Have you noticed in the modern drama
Its curious dependence on the telephone?
It's always ringing off-stage and on-stage,
A stage business to distract the audience,
Close some phase, or open to speculation.
It seems a cheap trick. We will have none of it.

C. A.

It aroused my curiosity.

Author

                            I am game
For female poets who shoot me in the ears.
I wish I were less civilized, a willing
Pander, for when they bring me their poems,
And I look into their eyes furtive or vindictive,
And see the nimble motions of their perturbed spirits,

I forthwith send their poems to publishers,
Whether they are good, bad, or donsense willables.

C. A.

You snipped that from my rack of private jokes.

AUTHOR

Ah, yes, how many subtleties of linguistic
I have learned from you. Remember the old days,
The free days of wearing gowns and riding bicycles,
When we used to drop in on A. E. Housman?
My Greek's all gone that once I dared to wax
On "Q" at evening Aristotle class.
We raced to heaven on ambiguities.

C. A.

You were swifter in the European fields
Of action, I recall. You astounded us.
Always in the front of some epic adventure.

AUTHOR

We never considered in those riant days
How much society determined us.
We were thrown up on the massive shoulders
Of our fathers, spume of the American wave.
We never considered the costive gilt of cash.

C. A.

You were a throw-back to the Romantics.

AUTHOR

You were a scientist of the succinct.

C. A.

You were plagued by jural mountains.

AUTHOR

You controlled and drilled gaiety.

C. A.

Our meeting was fortuitous and refreshing.

AUTHOR

A fort of friendship two decades abuilding.

C. A.

But now you wish to devise, and then to expedite
Some insoluble, or soluble, but resounding actions?

AUTHOR

Exacerbation of the inelastic essences.

C. A.

Purity of character is not a trick of words.

AUTHOR

> To be true to the true is to fight anew.
> A true revolutionary play would do away
> With action! Pure thought! Poetry could be
> A good deal of talk and dole of pure
> Intelligence, the largeness of the imaginative
> Act limited only to the receptivity
> Of the gustatory sensibility. Crop on the good.
> Make a picnic of reality.
> America is a hamburger mentality,
> But, for all that, the world is a handsome salad
> To be digested for a dance in the sun.
> We want the whole view of life. For what
> Is so monstrous as the fantastical
> Vanity of specialists? What so perfervid
> As the oblique lookers, encamped in slants?

C. A.

> You warm, and are heating up the tracks.

AUTHOR

> I want to know the truth, and know myself.
> I have seen Death himself, in his white robe,
> The king of shadows of a painless world,
> Walk in the gardens of the evening
> Spreading a dream of gold and amethyst
> Beyond our knowledge. His face was pure, and white.
> And I have seen Love, the equal partner
> Of the world, unmoving, a Madonna of the Rocks,
> In the full flesh of breasts and hips,
> The principle of nurture and of solace,
> Mother who gives the gift of birth;
> And mostly as I looked she represented purpose.

C. A.

> What do you intend to do about it?

AUTHOR

> That, Strong Staff, is what I am consulting you for.

C. A.

> I said I thought I could not be of much help.

AUTHOR

> Your modesty was ever excessive, urbane, and divisive.
> What do you think should be a theme for a play?
> I always wished to show off pussy Job,
> Nature's knobby, protuberant sufferer,
> And listen to his wails all day and night,

Sunk within that writhing, red conception,
But our old Jewish cultural ancestors
Eased his stance; for me unhappily;
He died happy, outlasting the surgeon steel
And idiom of a stark, accusing fortune
That tried to probe the stubborn man to death.
His masochism is not subtly suitable
For the locking song; he was the accused,
Not the accuser; and in that brainless forfeit
Foregoes the right to fall from seeming grace
By some dark flaw within himself revealed
In actions willed that bring on massive doom.

C. A.

Then why not present him as a Comic figure?

Author

Vitamins A, B, C, X, Y, and Z,
A few kind pills that any doctor gives,
Would fix him up and stop his baby crying,
A girlish dose to change the writhing feature,
And incidentally snake and take him
Altogether out of religious literature.

C. A.

You have something there. We know too much,
To make a laughing stock of Job with pills.
Can't you argue something psychosomatic
And bring in Freud and Jung as artisans
To aid?

Author

                    They are two modern Devils
Who set themselves as self-appointed gods,
The playboys of our intellectual weakness.
When the weakness of our characters
Shows in the meshes of complex reality,
And when we totter from ability,
They stare at us, imputing monstrous sins
And pustules of our insecurity,
They stare us down with methodology
And keep us down in hypnotic happiness
Presuppositional of greater knowledge
Would tell us what to do, and make us well.
Why, who should be so weak as to go to them?
Recline on their horse-hair shirt divans; sunk

To let them fish some spineless murex up
For all the gallant jewels of our natures?

C. A.

It is the fashion of the confused times.
All do. Their sway and suasion is liturgical.

Author

Your term is not well taken: their liturgy
Is limited to some dubious picture
Of a passionless, contemporary society
Where all, good people, get along together,
As if there were some absolute in reach,
A social norm, a just society;
Ease the shocks, accept the social patterns,
Stand in new love, and kiss the status quo.

C. A.

If they are pragmatical utilitarians
We should be wise to be latitudinarians.

Author

Yes, but we want a protagonist, and actions.

C. A.

Had you considered the Oedipus mythology?

Author

Yes, I was coming to that. Oedipus is never
Old hat; the notion is neat, round and pat.
But can we put him in a modern plot?
Aristotle is right to stress the plot,
But where have we any inevitability?

C. A.

Are you going to take a poke at Soph?

Author

To our new and Freudian sense, our apostatic
Defamation of the ancient character,
It seems abrogative to reach for Oedipus
And feel the vital Aristotelian tenets.
Pity and fear, indeed; the scholars' definitions
Thereof, endless excitations of the mind,
Elicitations of the text, weighted arguments.
But we are purged no more, think not on it.
Such transvaluations of the senses are
As to traduce the old dome of Sophocles.
His Oedipus is not a dark tragedian,
But happiest wisher. Rejoice! A man who killed
His father! A man who married his own mother!

This is the man who makes us laugh and dance,
This is the master of modern happiness.

C. A.

I think you approve extremist actions
Precisely because we have no frame or plot
To put them in making them inevitable.
They exemplify the swishing will you like.

AUTHOR

I always smelled a rat in the mother. Just think!
To marry your mother without knowing it,
Or, too, without her knowing it, despite
Of times, of treacheries, is hardly possible,
It always seemed to me. A loophole there.
I'll bet he knew it all the time, and loved it.

C. A.

A wicked stroke. You'd make him wicked by will?

AUTHOR

Wickeder by will than by just fate.

C. A.

Had you considered the Christ theme?

AUTHOR

It has long been pre-empted by the Mass.
I would like to show Christ-like actions.

C. A.

Maybe something of the conscientious objectors?

AUTHOR

A noble thing in prison it is to suffer
The wings and sparrows of outrageous torsion.
To try to stop the madness of mankind
By purity of heart; by their radical example
Opposing the ancient servitude of Cain
And saying in simple but formidable fashion
"I will not kill," as literally to explicate
The serene text of the loving certitude
And give their lives away, if any see,
By example, the folly of crimson, stuttering guns,
O that is a young simplicity and straightness
Marvelous in these times of massive argument
And hatred, denying even the cynic sophists
Who find in scripture anything to please them,
As, who argue, "I bring not peace, but a sword"
To justify the bayonet ways of man to man.

C. A.
> You might present a startling case.

AUTHOR
> Startling, all right. I'd show a moral youth
> Fired to the hilt with love, an active pacifist,
> Strong willed, courageous, highly educated,
> Who'd put himself before a war-time court,
> Stand up against the whole warring Government,
> Call in their lawyers and their hatchet men
> And show the spirit of Christ was living yet.

C. A.
> What happens next?

AUTHOR
>   O that's where Comedy
> Comes in.

C. A.
>   How so, in just what way?

AUTHOR
> Why, when this perfectionist protagonist
> Had subpoenaed the heads of the Selective Service
> And caused such intellectual scenes in court
> That they had to call in six lawyers to deal
> With him, and when the power of his spiritual fervor
> And passionate utterance of the rights of man,
> His moral strength, his clean, blue, astonishing eyes
> Had searched their vast authority for a week,
> The Judge, I suppose a man kind to children,
> Directs then to the jury of his peers
> The only and pale words that he could utter:
> Yes, peers, this man is morally just,
> Demonstrating to our inner shame
> That all who make and further wars are wrong,
> Culpable, and weak, not strong as seems.
> Yet, gentlemen, the enemy is reality,
> There is no time for ideality,
> We are at war: I charge you, lock him up.
> And when these peers had turned in the verdict Guilty,
> Sheep-like croppers of a bloody fodder,
> The Judge sentences him to four stark years
> In the Federal penitentiary,
> The maximum time for his impertinence
> And slander of the god and Moloch war.

C. A.
> That might make arresting spectacle.
> Have no special pleading for the audience,
> Deliver the complex facets of the scenes
> With capable disinterest.

Author
>   I'd keep it clean.
> Law makes long spokes of the short stakes of man.
> I'd try to get the absolute in the relative.

C. A.
> Keep away from vague generalities.

Author
> By being specific, I'd engage thus totalities.
> (*The phone rings*)
> Pardon me. Maybe it is another she.
> (*He goes to the phone*)
> Hello, yes, this is he. (*A pause*). Well, isn't that fine.
> I'm delighted. May I come on Thursday? Good.
> Congratulations, felicities. What great good luck.
> (*Returns to chair*)
> Another child has come upon the earth
> Trailing clouds of glory from occlusions of
> Caesarian birth.

C. A.
>   He'll push us off the boards,
> He'll see us out another way.

Author
>   We'll go down
> The Druid caverns to the icy wells,
> We'll walk in shadows in a silent time,
> Before he sees mid-day.

C. A.
>   It is getting late.
> I have to keep a date with scholarship
> Tomorrow. I'm afraid I haven't helped you much.
> Thank you for inviting me to your troubles.

Author
> A great fear and throe of oppressing time
> Weighs on me. Before the next generation comes
> To see the world, this universal spectacle,
> As hurling waters of the wrathful seas,
> And man the drowned, with his clothes torn off,
> And stitches the ragged coat of mankind up

With such whole love as it may have or find
We'll be hobgoblins in the unimproving slime,
With what we wanted most to say, unsaid.

C. A.

Well, don't take it too seriously.
Impress yourself that life's a kindling Comedy.
Will you treat of love?

Author

                    Yes, we'll treat of love,
That strange affliction.

C. A.

                    And jest upon it?

Author

As it is a digestible comestible.
It is a yeasty and jesty matter.
Go to it, go to it. Two by two
Makes the winy world both fair and true.

C. A.

                                        You talk
Like every man.

Author

                    I'll be a very man.
But I will love the world no less
Because of one in a salad dress.

C. A.

Love's the prettiest game of all, maybe.

Author

Maybe so, you ought to know, you devil.

C. A.

I thought you were the Devil?

Author

                              The Devil
I am.

C. A.

                    I always thought you angelical
To spout so much nonsense so seriously.

Author

Let us tear our pleasures with rough strife—

C. A.

Now it is through the hates of life.

Author

Remember the time we took that luminous girl
In my old green Pontiac for a whirl?

C. A.

We only got as far as Asbury Park.

Author

Silly to sleep on the sand in the dark.

C. A.

Under dunderheaded pilons, too.

Author

The tide came up to her pretty shoe.

C. A.

She loved neither you nor me, really.

Author

That's what made it delightful, a folly.

C. A.

She was a symbol of the chase.

Author

What a pregnant spirit in her face.

C. A.

It was all pretty ridiculous.

Author

She took the measure of both of us.

C. A.

She kept us at a striving distance.

Author

I wonder what has become of her now.

C. A.

Maybe regretting another prowess.

Author

One more word, before you go.

C. A.

What now?

Author

About the style. Should we make it
Fluid and florid, in full verbal spate
To touch on tongue ten thousand times,
As it were, the richness of our English,
Organ of shifting, grassy syllables,
Or taste of rich and savage splendors
Which, like the blood itself, that feeds
The tongue, come out to tell the world

All's a lush hectic in our English.
O sainted language (a Frenchman said that),
A peach with fuzz on it, most pure vowels
And bells of sound, hillside consonants,
What marriage to man's loves you have
To heighten pleasure and communicate
The supple rigors of the soul.

C. A.

                          Beware,
For in such heady, tigerish deportment
Your opulence may burst the learned bounds
Of reason, and take the mind on manic flights
Where sense and sensibility do not jell.

Author

You want a safe and sound control, sweet law
Of balanced harmonies, nothing excessive.
But I would mix, as on a painter's marble
Palette, the boldest colors of the earth
And paint upon the page, with lusty violence
All the dynamic energies of the age
That would burst forth in natural compulsions
Fruiting the eye with the vigors of the earth.

C. A.

Another style would be more daring now,
The spare, the lean, the chaste, a Greek
Of Doric, pure and strong restraint,
Where reason and imagination
Stay in sculptured elegance.
Try such strong discipline, such love
As holds back passion while it gives it.
None will deplore your study, all
Love harmony of sense and sound.

Author

Well, we'll see. One does the best one can
To bottle up and stock the spirit of man.
What about the language of the common man?

C. A.

That's fit for prose, not fit for poetry.

Author

As man is prosy, at times poetical,
Perhaps a stab at usual, practical talk,
With elevations here and there of poetry?

C. A.
>Do as you wish, just keep the Greeks in mind.
>Perhaps your spirit will find a new amalgam.

Author
>I will keep my style quite American.
>I'll call you when I have some brave confection.

C. A.
>I'll be delighted. Strive toward perfection.
>Good-bye, and thanks a lot again.

Author
>   So long
>Until the world shall open, and we shall spin.
>(*Motioning him back*)
>O, come back a minute, just a minute.
>Let us talk some more about style.
>(*C. A. turns back*)

C. A.
>   Have you
>Just imagined a new, a revolutionary one?

Author
>No. It's advantageous to talk about it
>Long after you have forgotten the ancients
>And all you have read on it.

C. A.
>   It's close to life,
>You mean?

Author
>   I guess I mean somewhat like that.
>It's all you've known and felt since you were little,
>All you have thought, and all you've dreamed to be.
>There is an idiom native to me, as American;
>My forebears, since they came in 1720,
>Rise up from wasting graves marked or unmarked
>To meet upon my tongue an immortality
>In meshes of the hungers of the living
>For life, more life; rich, brimming realizations.

C. A.
>Your bete-noire was ever a dedicated spirit
>Never far removed from the religious.
>Keep your preaching forebears out of it,
>I'd say. Depict the present time.
>Don't get to feeling you're oracular.

AUTHOR

        I'll try to be the disinterested receiver
        Of sometime messages and strategems,
        To entertain my ego toward quiescence.

C. A.

        Maybe you had better forget the whole affair.
        It seems to trouble you, to make you nervous.

AUTHOR

        The world would welcome another scientist.

C. A.

        Let's not engage that argument. The wise
        Are those who know their way about the world,
        Do what they can, and make the best of it.
        If the age is bruited against the artist
        The greater the challenge to his artistry.
        By imagination mine the deepest schist.
        So long, again.

AUTHOR

                I'm afraid that I have bored you,
        Not quite to death.

C. A.

                I feel death may come yet.
        Farewell.

                (Curtain)

The Apparition

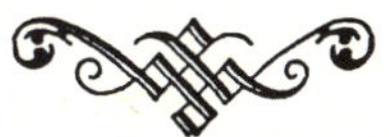

The Apparition

CHARACTERS: *Robin Everyman, Beryl Everyman, Jason Curley, Wendy Curley, Charlie Westgate, Grayce Westgate, Young Girl.*

SCENE: *The living room of the Everymans, with a small room beyond. Robin and Beryl are alone.*

ROBIN

I thought our last group play came off pretty well.

BERYL

I did too. What will we do tonight?
(A knock at the door. Enter, Jason and Wendy, Charlie and Grayce)

ROBIN

Hello, come in.

BERYL

                Hi, nice to see you.
(Sounds of hello, hello)

JASON

Scholarship is so exhausting. I am tired of footnotes.
What are we going to have tonight?

WENDY

                              I would like it
light.

GRAYCE

And something spicy.

CHARLIE

                We all want frothy fun.

ROBIN

Beryl, get some drinks.
(She goes to get drinks. They take seats in the living room, making small talk. Beryl returns, serves beer in mugs)

ROBIN

Tonight we have a quickie—Our last was heavy—

A little picture of an impish situation.
Shall we get on?
(*Cries of assent*)   Your eagerness is disarming.
We need a bed in this one. Charlie, Jason,
Lend a hand.

CHARLIE   Why, sure.

JASON   OK, that's easy.
(*They move a divan onto the inner stage at the end of the room,
    then reseat themselves*)

ROBIN

All else we need is a lissom apparition.
I will be the Everyman, the protagonist, myself.
The scene is a hotel bedroom, in a large,
Midwestern city. It is midnight. John,
We will call him, is sitting up in bed, writing.
I'll put on no disguise, think me now John.
(*He goes to the bed, first making an exit to reappear in night
    clothes. He is sitting up in bed in pajamas and dressing
    gown*)

JOHN

I guess I will write my wife before retiring.
(*He begins to write, writes a page, speaks*)
My dear sweet Chuck, I have done four hundred miles,
Am now propped up in bed, nerves reiterating
The candor of the day-end, unstable roadbed,
Midnight is growing slowly to be helpful,
I'll soon see you, I am restive to be with you—
(*There are three short knocks on the door. Robin stumbles out
    of bed, goes to the door in his pajamas and dressing gown, a
    natural gesture of one expecting nothing, or something per-
    functory. A young girl abruptly insinuates herself into the
    partially opened door, enters*)

ROBIN
Well?

GIRL

                  Well here I am. May I come in?

JOHN

You are in, it seems. Or am I having a nightmare?
(*She is young, thin, rather high-strung, but pliable and eager
    in manner*)

GIRL

I am having such a bad time. May I sit down?

JOHN

Why, I suppose so. Have that chair over there.
This is quite extraordinary. You're pretty—

GIRL

That is what they all say: actually, I am not.
At least nobody thinks so at the Post Office.

JOHN

What do you do at the Post Office, play Post Office?

GIRL

I don't know what you mean. I work there, of course.
They have had a lot of extra girls during the war.

JOHN

(Going back to bed, somewhat embarrassedly, sitting up in bed)
How old are you?

GIRL

                    Going on twenty, what do you
think?

JOHN

I thought I had done all my thinking for the day.
What can I do for you? Do you want a drink?

GIRL

I never drink much; my mother says it is a bad thing.
(John goes to bathroom, pours out two whiskeys and water)

JOHN

Here, take this. It will cheer you. You seem unhappy.
Do you live here?

GIRL

                    Of course I live here, have all my
life.

JOHN

Does your family live here too?

GIRL

                              My mother is left;
An older sister who is married and has kids.
(They drink)

JOHN

I am just passing through. I've driven all day.

GIRL

Why don't you stay for a while? It's a good town.

JOHN

Well, that's very nice of you. I have other things
to do.

47

GIRL

You seem to be a nice sort. Mind if I talk?
(He goes over and takes hold of her, and brings her over to the
    bed, where she half reclines, holding distance)

JOHN

We might dispense with talk. You have soft skin.
Have you ever done anything like this before?

GIRL

Say, what do you take me for?
(She repulses a minor advance)
                                        I'm feeling fine.

JOHN

Don't you think this is a dangerous thing to do?

GIRL

What if I scream. They'd have you in a minute.

JOHN

I had thought of that, of course, some time ago.
You interest me. You seem troubled. What is it?

GIRL

It's my ancestors. They are trying to destroy me.
Sometimes they come through my window in the night.

JOHN

You look Irish.

GIRL

                            That's it. I guess they all were.
I've never had any happiness at all.

JOHN

You seem somewhat fiery, rebellious, proud.
Come here, let me soothe you a little. It's quiet.
(He pulls her to him; she rises defiantly, goes to other side of the
    room, sits in a chair)

GIRL

You are all alike. I've just been reading Robinson Jeffers.
You're vile, you are vile, all of you, vile.

JOHN

Do you read much poetry?

GIRL

                                        He's the only one
I ever read.

JOHN

                        How did that happen, then?

48

GIRL

> Never mind. I like him, I read all night
> sometimes.

JOHN

> What did you come in here for?
> Didn't you think it would be dangerous?

GIRL

> Who cares for danger? Do you think I am a fool?
> I'm bored. I've been bored since eight o'clock.
> I was at a party downstairs in the dining room.
> My boy friend bores me to death. I can't escape him.
> He's always taking me out to dinners and dancing.

JOHN

> Would you like a little more to drink?

GIRL

> Well, maybe.
> *(He pours two more drinks, gets back into bed)*

JOHN

> Take it easy, now, take it easy.

GIRL

> I just couldn't stand it another minute.
> I said to myself, I'm going to take the elevator
> And go to the thirteenth floor. Then I'll get out,
> Turn to the right, walk down three rooms,
> Knock on the door three times, and see what happens.

JOHN

> I must say, you are rather adventurous.
> What if it had been an old lady deaf in one ear?

GIRL

> I'd leave, mumbling that I had made a mistake.

JOHN

> What if it had been a man younger than I, a wild one?

GIRL

> I don't know. I like talking with you, though.

JOHN

> I confess I am not given to this sort of thing.

GIRL

> Say, you talk funny. What are you anyway?

JOHN

> I'm traveling, and took this hotel room for the night.
> You seem much quieter now, your nerves are eased,
> The drink has done you good, I'm glad you came,

As I was feeling nervous. I now feel fine.
But wouldn't you like to make a little love,
Maybe just a little?

GIRL

                                    You are all alike,
I hate love. It makes me sick in the stomach.

JOHN

Do you know anything about it?

GIRL

                                            My mother told me.
I have to be careful because of confession.

JOHN

O, so you're a Catholic. That makes a difference.

GIRL

O, what shall I do? I am very much upset
And I must decide by Saturday. It is unnerving.

JOHN

Good Heavens, what must you decide by then, by
    Saturday?

GIRL

Whether to become a nun.

JOHN

                                    No wonder you are perturbed.
Now whatever do you want to become a nun for?
You are young, and I think you quite attractive.

GIRL

The world is so cruel. My mother wants me to.
To take the veil is so pure and clean, a dream
I've had as I grew up. It is sweet and pure.
The world is so vile, it's all so vile, so vile.

JOHN

Do you understand what you are renouncing?

GIRL

I understand the glory I would find.

JOHN

It is a hard choice. I wish I could help you.
If that is what is troubling you, my dear,
It seems an odd thing that you are here.

GIRL

I can put them off for a month from Saturday.
I've never been South. I want to go to West Palm Beach.
I'm going there, I must, and lie in the sunshine,
And then I am going to decide, once for all.

JOHN

> I approve of your going South. A great deal of sun
> Would help you, I should think it might help a lot.

GIRL

> You are nice. But I must go. It must be getting late.

JOHN

> Don't hurry away.

GIRL

>   Say, if you ever come again
> I'd like to have you out to the house. Here is
> My address. We could sit on the porch swing.

JOHN

> That is rather a sweet thought. Thank you so much.
> Maybe our paths will cross again some time.

GIRL

> Good night. Good-bye.

JOHN

>   Good-bye. Good night.
> *(She leaves)*
> They all get burned sooner or later, sun or man.
> *(Pause)*
> Take care of this Thy servant, O Son of Man.
> *(Takes up his letter again in bed, writes, then reads)*
> Long drives alone were not for such as your
> Lover, haunted by midnight dreams of beauty.
> It is the witching hour of night, I'll see you soon.

(Curtain)

JASON

> A quickie. Bogged in the love of peat.

GRAYCE

> No play, if she had been five years older.

CHARLIE

> She would be played on in another way.

ROBIN

> The play's the sting.

BERYL

>   A very light play bill.

CHARLIE

> The audience would want more billing and wooing.

ROBIN

> I tell you this is pure imagination
> And that it is absolute reality.

JASON

> He's Irished it. Bogged down for the love of peat.
> It is really the blue flower of Novalis.

CHARLIE

> A touch of Everyman.

JASON

> A very man.

ROBIN

> Jones Very?

CHARLIE

> Very good. A Very light.

JASON

> A touch of Everyman makes all men sin.
> It is the thinnest theater we are in.
> Haven't you a poem, Charlie, about women?
> The one that came out in the Specific Director.
> Let us have meat to this sauce and season.

ROBIN

> Women are a meaty matter.

WENDY

> Does he reason well?

ROBIN

> I recall his women as digestible.

CHARLIE

> I have a poem called "An Emblem of Viable Women."

JASON

> Pentametric? Hexametric?

GRAYCE

> If he is telling the truth I got him just in time.
> He never could keep a woman off his line.

CHARLIE

> If you will all quiet down a little, I'll read it.

BERYL

> We are souls of decorum. We are pure tact.

CHARLIE

> *(Showing a fit of artistic temperament)*
> No, I'm not in good voice. I'm nervous, nerves
>   dancing.

WENDY

> On that sober note we had better go home.
> *(They all make gestures of leave-taking)*

JASON

My fleeces need attending to.

CHARLIE

                                        I'm hydroptic.

GRAYCE

Let's go home. Soon you'll be barbituritic.
I'll fix you. Robin, you are a lithe devil,
I think you are positively angelical.

ROBIN

A duellist of the schizophrenic unity.

BERYL

His duel is to keep himself being dual.

ROBIN

Dualism henceforth always be my rule.

CHARLIE

And tool.

WENDY

                        And fuel.

JASON

                        And stool.

ROBIN

                                My fool, my jewel.
*(They seem to weave back into the room in a kind of rhythmic
dance as if their enthusiasm for the evening's performance
needed a unifying, unified ritual, which they grow into quickly
and formally. They surround Robin in formal attitudes
making a half-circle about him as they develop and perfect
the following routine)*

GRAYCE

You're a scream.

WENDY

                You're a dream.

ROBIN

I'm a filibuster.

JASON

                You're a huckster.

CHARLIE

A bit of a mucker.

ROBIN

                Hugger-mugger.

JASON

You're a Parliamentarian.

53

CHARLIE

You're an alimentarian.

GRAYCE

You're a Platypusarian.

ROBIN

I'm Eleemosynarian.

GRAYCE

Boo.

WENDY

Who?

BERYL

You?

ROBIN

True.
Let's keep it light and gay
And whisk dull capers away.

JASON

And tittivate tractarians.

WENDY

And diagnose Sumerians.

CHARLIE

Accept rights riparian.

GRAYCE

Occlude notes totalitarian.

BERYL

Engender fanfaroles and catch at catches.

ROBIN

Chortle at midnight, raise all the latches.

WENDY

And sing.

BERYL

And wing.

JASON

And ping.

CHARLIE

A ring around
Capable treasure.

BERYL

Surfeitless pleasure.

ROBIN

A true dance
measure.

54

GRAYCE

    Nonsense.

JASON

            Is don sense.

CHARLIE

                 Pretense!

ROBIN

                    Common sense

    Investigator.

JASON

         Imitator.

WENDY

             Hexter.

BERYL

               Prevaricator.

ROBIN

    Theatrical.

WENDY

        Syntactical.

CHARLIE

            Magical.

BERYL

              A madrigal.

ROBIN

    Fantastic.

WENDY

        Grammatic. Pragmatic.

CHARLIE

              Astigmatic.

ROBIN

    Spasmodical.

WENDY

        Rhapsodical.

CHARLIE

           Angelical.

BERYL

              Coromandelical.

JASON

    Sal Hepatica!

WENDY

        Bovrillity.

CHARLIE

                      Nux Vomica!

ROBIN

                                   Coca-Cola.

BERYL

    Poet.

JASON

        Painter.

GRAYCE

          Musician.

ROBIN

             Priest.
We are all going up in a cloud of yeast,
A land of yeast and fevers of the Beast.
(They all calm down, finally standing still)
Another time we'll stalk another stance
And search out man in his deceiving dance.
And if you'll be our loves, and come with me,
Since we feel tragical, we'll try another comedy.

The Visionary Farms

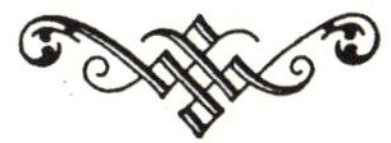

The Visionary Farms

Scene I

CHARACTERS: *Robin Everyman; Beryl Everyman, his wife; Jason Curley, a scholar, formerly the Consulting Author; Wendy Curley, his wife; Charlie Westgate, a scholar, also a poet; Grace Westgate, his wife.*

SCENE: *Home of the Everymans.*

ROBIN

Well, here we are for another thrust
And joust against man's ancient adversary.

CHARLIE

What is that, this time?

ROBIN

        The death of his spirit.
For if he has not imaginative fire
He is as good as gone.

CHARLIE

       Gone where?

ROBIN

           Why,
Gone to the devil.

JASON

     Are you still the Devil?

ROBIN

A prince of great price, somewhat angelical.
I'd be a devil to flay his death-like spirit,
An angel to illuminate the affair man.
So let us, in our present enterprise,
Turn time backward, to see what powers,
Forces, circumstances, and chances
Burgeon and develop in a situation,
And tread a little, within our theater,
Some baffled steps of the journey of Everyman.

JASON
          I am prepared to order my imagination.
WENDY
          Is it going to be a comedy?
ROBIN
          Wendy, if you have studied definitions
          Practically everything is. We will show
          The strong, pervasive reaches of the world,
          Conjure a time of massive brightness,
          Elicit the hammering flaws, and what time does.
CHARLIE
          This sounds pretty serious.
GRAYCE
                              I had hoped
          You would make it light and racy.

ROBIN
          The past may show an eternal present.
JASON
          Take fortune in strong gripe, and break its neck?
WENDY
          That is fantastical.
BERYL
                         We are bound
          On Fortune's wheel. It is not bound by us.
          It is always good to gain perspective
          In viewing a universal spectacle.
WENDY
          What, universal in a little room?
BERYL
                                   An everywhere.

GRAYCE
          Let's go.
CHARLIE
                         As if we had not life enough,
          We must relive and tempt it forth in imitation.
BERYL
          And open our souls to truth's old worst.
ROBIN
          You talk as if you had not known of it.
GRAYCE
          Of what?

ROBIN

                    We are mincing tricksters. Summer's gone.
You have had the blithe, the budding time,
The time of blossoms, then the burning time
To learn your parts by now. Cast off the quotidian
And let us deal with an American scene.

BERYL

The pool of memory, and of our large desire.

JASON

I confess I have not learned my part or parts.
I had to screw the lid on Henry James.
It took all summer with a silver screwdriver.

WENDY

My work on Spanish folklore was exacting.
I am mainly interested in the thirteenth century.
After that, history is not good repetition.

ROBIN

I suspected this. I coped with it.

GRAYCE

Spock and Gesell have exercised my time,
Along with a brace of brassy gynecologists.

CHARLIE

I had to force a course on Melville; Moby Dick
Swallowed me entire. I am pure whiteness.

ROBIN

This is to laugh. It is comedy
Before it begins. We are the comedians
Who do not take our theater seriously,
Arguing that upon our several stages
We like to play our own realities
Compelled by egotistical esteems.
Beryl, could you make us all a drink?
We will sit around and pass the glass of time.
(There is a knock at the door. Robin lets in Consulting Author)
Good evening. You came in just at the right time.
You know all of these people, I believe?

CONSULTING AUTHOR

How do you do. It is good to see you again.

ROBIN

Come in, sit down.
(Beryl brings drinks)
                    Here is a glass with whisky.
I want to consult with you, seriously.

CHARLIE
    The waters of life.
BERYL
                                        Would you have charged water?
CONSULTING AUTHOR
    It is pleasant to think I might be helpful.
    (Beryl passes drinks all around)
    Thank you.
GRAYCE
                        Thank you.
WENDY
                                    Thank you.
CHARLIE
                                        Thank you.
JASON
                                            Thanks.
ROBIN
    My desire is to show an impossible situation.
CONSULTING AUTHOR
    Make it probable. Everything is probable.
ROBIN
    It is so real people would not believe it.
CONSULTING AUTHOR
    Then you would not have to invent it. Seeing
    Is believing.
ROBIN
                        I always thought seeing was deceiving.
CONSULTING AUTHOR
    Legerdemain and sleight-of-hand are handy.
    As a matter of fact, I have powers of divination.
ROBIN
    I always suspected you of being a devil.
CONSULTING AUTHOR
    I am also somewhat angelical.
    I have been operating by thought-transference
    Now for quite some time, with respect to you.
ROBIN
    Why, this is astonishing.
CONSULTING AUTHOR
                        In fact it is.
ROBIN
    Do you not think I know what I want to do?

CONSULTING AUTHOR

> You see as through a glass, darkly. Everyone does,
> Almost. I have special powers of divination.
> I will show you what you wish to show.

GRAYCE

> This is weird. What is he going to do?

WENDY

> It sounds strange.

BERYL

> Not table-lifting, I trust.

JASON

> I am waiting to see the accustomed rabbit.

CHARLIE

> I would not mind a new kind of parlor trick.
> *(Consulting Author goes swiftly to the door, lets in six young
> men actors, three young women. They nod, but do not speak.
> They stand around in professional ease)*

CONSULTING AUTHOR

> I have conjured these, my sprites, from Harvard Square.
> They will actuate my airy theater.
> If you do not mind our using your other room
> We will pass before your eyes some tricks.
> The girls will set the stage. Women are always
> Setting stages. I will be the director,
> And you can be the drinking spectators.
> Whenever necessary, I'll be a commentator.
> Drink in our merry and sometime festive clarity.
> *(At Consulting Author's motion of command the actors go out
> right, reappearing only on stage later as action indicates. The
> six principals sit as if somewhat spellbound, anticipating and
> ready for what may transpire.
> Consulting Author takes a wand out of his inner breast pocket.
> He makes a few passes over the six principals)*
> I carry a delicate, mystic, silken wand
> To clear the air on these cloudy occasions.
> I wave this now before your eyes and minds
> To purge the qualities of every day,
> And take your disbelieving personalities.
> Each thus becomes a part of Everyman.
> What is, is what might happen to him.
> And each can share in the scenes of fabulous life
> As if imagination were reality,
> For reality is strange as imagination.

(He puts down his wand on a table)
Now I must become a barker. Come all,
Come to see our show, our spectacle,
No furtive side show; big tent events.
The time is 1919. The place,
A small town in the Middle West.
The scene is in the Congregational church;
Within it a little Sunday School.
Thompson Ransome will soon appear,
That shrewd, expansive citizen
Noted as a most quick character
Who will teach the growing youth.

SCENE II

SCENE: *The Congregational Church.*
>   *(Ransome comes into the stage room, dark, dapper, serious,*
>   *about 35. He stands behind a flat desk upon which are two*
>   *glasses. Several boys and girls come in after him. They take*
>   *seats)*

RANSOME
>   Now boys and girls, I want you to sit still.
>   I am going to talk about good and evil.
>   We all want you to be good boys and girls,
>   Grow up to be a credit to our town,
>   Go out and do something in the world
>   Worthy of note, and of our care.
>   You have to be good to do good.
>   You must develop stalwart wills
>   To resist temptation and evil.
>   You must develop the fierce strength
>   And maintain the ceaseless vigilance
>   Of our fathers who came to this West country
>   To build anew the American dream.
>   Do not deviate from the truth,
>   Follow the harsh light of its gleam.
>   Do not lie, steal, be bullies or be mean.
>   Obey your parents and your teachers.
>   Work hard in school, labor diligently
>   To grow up straight, to better your minds.
>   There is no end to what you can do.
>   The world is a wealth of opportunity,
>   If you will do good, and shun evil.
>   But woe unto you if you do evil.

I am going to show you an experiment,
Something that you will never forget.
Notice these filled glasses here.
I am going to take out a silver dollar.
(He takes a silver dollar from his right pocket)
Notice the brightness of this dollar.
See how clean it is, hard and pure,
A symbol of the American dream.
I will drop it in this glass of water.
(He drops it in a glass of water. The class is all attention.
Pause. After a minute he takes it out)
Here it is, I hold it up,
Bright, hard, pure and clean.
Now I will drop it in this glass.
(He drops it in a glass of transparent hydrochloric acid. Little
cries of astonishment as it turns black, fuming. The youths
are fascinated, somewhat spellbound at the trick. Ransome
holds the glass with the black dollar at the bottom right before
their faces)
See how it is black all over.
Where is its brightness and its cleanliness?
Where is its luster, its bright shining?
It is ugly and impure immediately.
(He takes the blackened dollar out with a pair of forceps from
his pocket and holds it before them, menacingly)
If you do good you will be a shining brightness,
The world will love you and respect you,
You will have a fair name among men,
You will honor your fathers and mothers
And honor your Father who is in Heaven.
If you do evil, your soul will turn black
Immediately, like this hideous dollar.
You will be ruined, ugly and unvaluable,
Of no shining use in the world,
Corroded and lost in damnation.
Do not sin. Do not do evil.
You have within you the power of free will
To be good, or to sink into black evil.
May you never forget this experiment.
Go, and do good. The class is dismissed.
(The youths sidle out, disturbed and much impressed. Ran-
some leaves with an air of rather prim satisfaction)

SCENE III

CHARACTERS: *Adam Fahnstock, secretary and vice-president of the Parker Corporation, large manufacturers of soaps; Vine Fahnstock, his wife; their children, William, 16, Peter, 15, Suzanne, 10.*

SCENE: *Sunporch of the new, large Fahnstock house. Adam is reading the Sunday paper.*

FAHNSTOCK

What did you learn in Sunday School this morning, Pete?

PETER

Mr. Ransome gave us a lecture on good and evil.

FAHNSTOCK

I trust you profited by the experience.

PETER

He put a dollar in a glass of water.
He put it in another, I guess sulfuric acid.
It turned black. Then he gave us a lecture.

FAHNSTOCK

I have always taught you boys to be honest.
There are three basic rules of life.
If you follow these you are bound to succeed.
Health, honesty, and hard work.
Never do anything to undermine
Your health; you have strong constitutions.
I have told you to be absolutely honest.
Never tell a lie. And always work hard.
That must have been an interesting lesson.
Ransome has proved a good man with money.

WILLIAM

I thought it was a little artificial.
He sounded almost like the minister

PETER

Bill, come and help me fix my bike.
The right pedal is bent.

WILLIAM

All right, I will.

(They leave, right)

VINE

Suzanne, don't you want to go in the kitchen
And watch Inga make the strawberry shortcake?

SUZANNE

>Yes, Mother.
>*(She goes out, left)*

VINE

>You said Mr. Parker was coming over?

FAHNSTOCK

>Roger said he would drop over for a visit.

VINE

>We must get the new Victrola fixed.
>I am anxious to hear the new Caruso records.

FAHNSTOCK

>Always something to fix. The new Cadillac
>Looks as if it would never break down, though.
>I am planning a new silo for the farms;
>We need another for the big barn.
>I think I will put in fifty new Holsteins.
>A bull named Piebe Laura Olley Homestead King
>Is on the market. He is worth twenty thousand dollars.
>Three of the men at the office each agree to take a fourth.

VINE

>I never could hold you down. You are too heady.
>I wanted a comfortable house, just large enough,
>Instead of this enormous mansion. Ten acres
>Of lawn is too much. I spend my energy
>Ordering the servants, instead of enjoying life.

FAHNSTOCK

>You know you love it. It has been my dream.
>Think of the success, Vine, we are enjoying
>Since the old days when we started on nothing.

VINE

>I tried to keep you from building the Mad House.

FAHNSTOCK

>That house at the bottom of the Grand Canyon
>Took my eye. I said I would never rest
>Until we had one like it on our forty acres
>Where the children could play, and for our picnics.
>Thick steaks sizzling over the open fireplace!
>Those two buffalo horns I had set in the cement
>That I got from Ranch 101 out in Kansas
>Are a nice touch. You know you love it all.

VINE

>I love you, but wish you were not so expansive.
>We have too much. It may spoil the children.

67

FAHNSTOCK

        I wanted more than anything in my life
        To give them this estate to grow up on,
        To give them everything that I did not have,
        And build in them such fundamentals of good character
        That they cannot but succeed in later life.

VINE

        Think of what we spent on the furniture
        And the interior decorators from New York.

FAHNSTOCK

        I wanted to have the finest house in town,
        Bar none. Now we have got it. Let's enjoy it.
        Of course, ours is not as grand as Mr. Parker's.

VINE

        Mr. Parker owns the Company
        You must never forget. I feel somewhat restive
        About all of these grandiose developments.

FAHNSTOCK

        Just think, I started from the bottom, on nothing.
        Now twenty years later, due to industry
        And hard work, I own thirty-five per cent of the stock.

VINE

        You must be careful, though, about the future.
        Son Ted will be coming back from Jefferson.
        His father will want him to go into the business.

FAHNSTOCK

        Young Ted? He's wild, and has shown no ability.
        Let us cross that bridge when we come to it.
        *(There is a knock on the door. Roger Parker enters, a tall, spare
            yet full-bodied, intelligent-looking man of 60, the president of
            the Company)*

PARKER

        Hello, Vine and Adam. It is a nice Sunday morning.

VINE

        The summer is lovely. How is Margaret?

PARKER

        She is not feeling very well, but nothing serious.
        I just thought I would drop over for a little visit.

FAHNSTOCK

        I was just telling Vine about our new plans
        To expand the farms, to put up a new silo,
        And put in another herd of Holsteins for milk.

PARKER

You have quite a place there, a going concern.
I have heard you have bought some adjacent property.

FAHNSTOCK

Yes, another parcel, two hundred and forty acres.
We will put it the first year into timothy.

PARKER

I never had any interest much in farms.
All you men seem to be going in for them
In a great way in the last few years.
Ransome is developing a chicken ranch
And has already got twenty thousand chickens.

FAHNSTOCK

He is certainly aggressive; and very sound.

PARKER

Yes, we made a wise move in selecting him.
He was always good at figures, from the first.
You remember, after he was out of business college,
That local one over in Hopkins, when he came to us,
I think I started him at twelve dollars a week.
I came out here from Ohio in 1898.
I was luckiest of all, two years later,
To get you, Adam. You've done a magnificent job;
But I never thought you would become a veritable genius
In promoting and selling the company's products
All over the country, developing branch facilities.
We partake of the greatness of America
And nothing can stop us.

FAHNSTOCK

                    Yes, it is wonderful
And you are the one with the original insight
Into the almost limitless possibilities.
We neither of us dreamed, not even you did,
That we would be grossing many millions in sales
When we began in that small old factory.

PARKER

I have had the greatest confidence
In Ransome as the comptroller of the treasury.
He has grown up with it as we have become big,
A very valuable man, thoroughly satisfactory.
He has a passion for modernizing farms, too.
He says he is managing them very profitably.

FAHNSTOCK

He is capable in handling the Company's money.
It is fortunate for both of us we developed him.

PARKER

He became so much interested in his work
That he will not take time off for a vacation.
That's real devotion. His farms being near at home
He has no trouble in managing and attending to them.

FAHNSTOCK

He has set up an office on Water Street
Where he now employs, I believe, twelve girls.

PARKER

He is interested in developing real estate.
I never objected to the apartment buildings
He put up last year, so long as they make money.
No wonder we like the nickname Hurricane Ransome;
Hurry for short. He is always speeding things up.

FAHNSTOCK

He is teaching my sons in the Sunday School.

PARKER

That is good. He was always a moral man.
We are all secure and we have nothing to fear.
I must leave now, just a friendly chat.
We are going up to the Lakes next week.

VINE

I hope you will catch a thirty-pound musky.

PARKER

I fish only to order my thoughts, and get a change.
Good-by.

VINE

My best to Margaret.

PARKER

Good-by, Adam, Vine.

(He turns back)
Another thing I recall about Hurricane.
Do you remember when he first came he was restless
On my twelve dollars a week. We had, I think,
About twenty-two hundred employees then.
Within two months, with his native inventiveness,
He was selling candy at lunch hour to the workers,
Which brought him in a substantial increase.

FAHNSTOCK

                                        He then
Set up a stand, and became very popular with them.
They all loved his speedy way of doing things,
Always in a rush to improve things all around.
He made as little profit as he could on each piece
But in doing it he had a lot of fun.

PARKER

Imagine his calling his place The Visionary Farms.
But as long as they pay, I guess it is all right.

GRAYCE

Men, by nature expansive and idealistic,
Think to know how to teach us the realistic.

WENDY

We are less hectic, and are skeptics.
But it is the great spring of wildness in the West.

GRAYCE

Why should he write with a library in mind?
What these men do every day is beyond belief.
They are advancing to a full complexity
Springing passionately out of their own breasts.
Life has more artistry than art itself.

WENDY

Something is coiled up here like a tiger
Will spring in the new year; that I suspect.
Whenever I have thought hard about mankind
It has been through some historical perspective.
I see that we live in the fevers of the real
And if we think too much, we have to laugh.
Is it not a laugh that all is Comedy?

GRAYCE

Nothing can be too realistic for me.
I have an appetite that calls for blood.

WENDY

No doubt all dollars are sulfuric.

SCENE IV

SCENE: *Office of the chicken ranch on The Visionary Farms.
Thompson "Hurricane" Ransome at his desk. An electric
fan is running. It is summertime, July. Hurricane is a man
of quick, energetic gestures, wiry, forceful, direct. He is
reading the local paper. He rings a buzzer. His manager,
Jones Taft, comes in.*

HURRY

Taft, this is a sweltering hot day.
I want these farms thoroughly modernized.
How would you like to be one of our cows?
I have to swat flies even in here.
They spend half of their energy swishing their tails
Trying to keep off the flies. I want action.
I want a master fan made with six-foot arms,
Here is a rough sketch.
(Shows a rough sketch)
                                    Notice the fine points.
Put plenty of power on it. Blow all the flies
Into and pen them in this metal corridor,
Like this. Set up these elements there
Where they will be automatically asphyxiated.

TAFT

I will try to have it made in a month, sir.

HURRY

A month! I want it done in a week.

TAFT

I'll try, sir.

HURRY

                        Also, I want an electric fan
For each cow.

TAFT

                        Very good, sir.

HURRY

                                    I want vacuum cleaners
To keep the cows immaculate, specially made
With heads to make them feel they are being massaged.

TAFT

We can probably get some blueprints from Chicago.

HURRY

Chicago, nothing. Adapt them. Have them made here.
I want them set up in a week.

TAFT

                                        I'll try it, sir.

HURRY

If you cannot manage the works to suit me
I will have to get somebody else who can.
How many were there here over the week end?

TAFT

We served free lunches to ten thousand, sir.

HURRY

       I spent ten thousand dollars on the children's pool.
       Was it full, too? Do they use the swimming pool?

TAFT

       It is full every day, sir, crowded Saturdays and Sundays.

HURRY

       It makes me sick and tired to procrastinate.
       When I started this chicken farm two years ago
       So many visitors came to see the ranch
       I had to have a hotel put up to take care of them.
       I told your predecessor to build one in two weeks.
       He couldn't oblige. I fired him and did it myself.
       I made the contractor put it up in two weeks,
       Including music room, library and billiard room.

TAFT

       And a very commodious place it is, sir.

HURRY

       How many chickens have we got now, all told?

TAFT

       Twenty thousand is the official count.

HURRY

       How many from Japan?

TAFT

                              Five hundred and fifty-five, sir.

HURRY

       How many from Brazil?

TAFT

                         A thousand, and as of yesterday, two.

HURRY

       What about the new cross breeds?

TAFT

                              Coming along nicely, sir.
       We are losing quite a few to an unknown disease.

HURRY

       What we need is a chicken physician and surgeon.
       Get on long distance, call the State University
       And see if you can locate just such a person.
       Tell him we will give him ten thousand a year.

TAFT

       Yes, sir.

HURRY

                         We can easily afford that for the right man.

I must have the best expert in the field
To take care of the prize I got from Java.
I paid ten thousand for that one rooster,
The finest bird in the world, to lead the flock.

TAFT

I will make the call, sir.
(He phones)

HURRY

                              Make the girl hurry it up.
The only way to make money is to spend money.
*(There is a knock at the door. An automobile salesman comes
    in)*

SALESMAN

Good day, sir.

HURRY

Good day. What do you want?

SALESMAN

I have a new eight-cylinder Cadillac outside
I would like to show you.

HURRY

                              What color is it?

SALESMAN

Blue.

HURRY

I'll take it, send it to my home at once.

SALESMAN

Don't you want to see it?

HURRY

                              What for? Good day, get out.
(Salesman goes out hurriedly. The manager returns)

TAFT

They are flying a chicken surgeon down right now.
They say he is the best in the field. The plane is doing ninety.

HURRY

How much money do we make on milk?
Maybe we had better put on some more herds
To feed the chickens. Is that new mash working well?

TAFT

Very well. We give a lot of our milk to the children.

HURRY

I want everybody in the country
To come and see The Visionary Farms.

I want to show them how we do business.
Look at that stack of letters three feet high,
Inquiries in only one day on our poultry
Which we now ship to every part of the country
For breeding purposes, or even send them abroad.
One of my best schemes was The Visionary Trail.
It will be done very shortly. I am having the V.T. insignia
In great gold and black letters painted on
Every telephone pole from Minneapolis to Chicago,
Deflecting the route to come through the ranch here.
I estimate a crowd of ten thousand on Sundays
And have built up a forty-piece saxophone band
To open up the new dance hall. Quick work,
Especially by the interior decorators from New York.
(He takes up the phone, dials a number)
Hello, is this the Valence Syndicate in St. Paul?
This is Thompson Ransome of The Visionary Farms.
Send five hundred dollars' worth of the finest linens
You have for my hotel here. I want them at once.
How should you send them? Why put them in a taxi
And get them here within three hours. Hurry it up.
*(He puts down telephone. There is a knock at the door. Enter
    chicken physician and surgeon)*

BEANPOLE

My name is Rubin Beanpole, to be your surgeon.

HURRY

Beanpole, listen to this.
(He picks up a letter from his desk)
                              We have twenty thousand
Chickens here, and letters are pouring in from all sides
With checks from every part of the United States
From people who want the Visionary product.
Here is a letter from a man in Kansas City.
He wants a prize-winning rooster to beat a friend
Of his. He says, "I'm willing to pay three hundred and fifty
And split the prize money with you if I get it."
I will take him up.
*(He rings a buzzer.
    Enter Taft)*

HURRY

                    Taft, go out among the flocks
And bring me the best prize-winning rooster we have.

TAFT

>Yes, sir.
>*(Leaves)*

HURRY

>Do you think you will like the job?

BEANPOLE

>The danger is to escape the natural plagues.
>Often some bug or other gets into them.
>It is something that destroys them from the inside.

HURRY

>It is your business to keep them looking fine.
>I will get somebody else if you can't keep them well.
>*(Taft brings back a handsome rooster)*
>Is that the best we have got? Like it, Doctor?
>*(Beanpole nods)*
>Well, this is a very handsome critter, but not
>Good enough. I am determined to win that bet.
>The comb is not of the proper sort. Alter it,
>Beanpole, alter it.
>*(Beanpole opens his case, like a doctor's kit, takes out surgical
>   instruments, alters comb to make it look bigger)*

HURRY

>The color is all wrong. Taft, get some bleach.
>*(Taft goes out, returns quickly with bleaching materials, hands
>   them to Beanpole)*

HURRY

>Well, bleach it, Beanpole, bleach it.
>*(Beanpole bleaches part of the rooster)*

BEANPOLE

>Now I think he is bleached to suit.

HURRY

>His tail!
>That is not the tail of the best prize winner.
>Taft, go out among the flocks; bring me the best
>Tail feathers off the best roosters you can find.

TAFT

>All right.
>*(Taft leaves. They admire the bird. He returns with a large
>   handful of feathers)*

HURRY

>Now, Beanpole, perform an operation
>On this critter and make his tail superlative.

Take these extra tail feathers, splice them
And glue them on, make him the handsomest bird,
Worthy of The Visionary Farms.
(Beanpole operates, splices and glues)

BEANPOLE

There, there, sir, there is your beauty.

HURRY

Well, maybe. I'll bet I'll win that bet.
Taft, crate him and send him right along to Kansas City.

TAFT

Very well, sir.

HURRY

                    That will be all for today.

WENDY

    Gaiety lifts the spirit to racy heights.

GRAYCE

    Realism makes me feel hot and frothy.

SCENE V

SCENE: *In Ransome's office at the chicken farm. One month
    later. Ransome is sitting at his desk. He presses a buzzer.
    Beanpole comes in.*

HURRY

Beanpole, our rooster won the grand first prize.
I knew we could put it over on them. Success is a trick.
I am giving you a thousand-dollar raise
Because of the success of your operation.

BEANPOLE

Thank you, sir. I need a new laboratory
To study the evidences of internal destruction.
There is some bug destroying them from the inside.

HURRY

Have one put up at once to your satisfaction.
Hire as many assistant experts as you like.
We want the land carpeted with chickens.
Don't let anything get them from the inside.
(Presses a buzzer. Taft comes in)
Taft, the insignia on the telephone poles
Directing the people to The Visionary Farms
Were completed almost at once.

TAFT

                                        Very good, sir.
HURRY

    How many came to the mammoth celebration
    When we opened the new dance hall last week?
TAFT

    We expected about ten thousand, sir,
    But we clocked in sixty thousand spectators.
HURRY

    Fine, fine. I could be here only an hour.
    Did Caruso sing?
TAFT

                        He did, he sang "O Solo Mio"
    Over the loudspeaker I set up.
    Everybody was wild about his singing.
    The multitude wanted you to give a speech, sir.
HURRY

    Speech, nothing. I am a man of action.
    What do you think I got the entertainers for?
    I ordered thirty special newspaper writers
    And twenty magazine writers to spread the word
    All over the country about The Visionary Farms.
TAFT

    They were much impressed, sir. Have you seen this?
    (He proffers a large rotogravure section setting forth in page
        after page the glories of The Visionary Farms)
HURRY

    Pretty good. Put it on the stack of them over there.
BEANPOLE

    I have to report that one of the prize roosters has died.
HURRY

    Died? That's impossible. What did you do to it?
BEANPOLE

    It is some bug boring from within, sir.
    It is something getting in the inside of them.
HURRY

    Which one? Not the Javanese Master, the Leader?
BEANPOLE

                                        Luckily not.
    It was the Starry Striker from Havana.
HURRY

    Beanpole, I am going to take away your raise.
    We do not want death and destruction here.

Futhermore, we have got to treat these birds right.
Taft, what we need is a chicken cemetery.
We are not just going to throw them away.
I want you to set up one on the Ridge lot.
Set up a twenty-ton marble monument;
Have carved on it, "In Rest, Our Feathered Friends."

TAFT

Yes, sir. I will have it carved in Carrara.

HURRY

Never mind Carrara. Get it from Vermont.
I want it all set up and placed in two weeks.
A kind of special park for our guests to walk in.
Have sculptures of cocks on marble pedestals.
I want you to install a loudspeaking system
Which can be turned on Saturdays and Sundays
Giving the recorded calls of twenty types of prize roosters.

TAFT

That will be quite lively, sir.

HURRY

                              That is what we want.
No death and destruction on The Visionary Farms.
We are showing the world how to manage life.
It is just as easy to have big ideas as little ones.
America is powerful, of limitless possibilities,
All it takes is speed and audacity.
Why, Hell's bells, it's easy, it's a cinch.

BERYL

    I grew up in a bright and furious time.

GRAYCE

    Nobody really knows what the times are like.

SCENE VI

SCENE: *Office of Hurry Ransome in the Parker Corporation.*
    He is alone.

HURRY

Sometimes I have to think out loud
To keep from sort of getting the creeps.
(He studies the Company's books and ledgers)
I always thought it was easy to juggle books
Since I studied them at Hopkins College.
These double entries balance and check off,
But they didn't think anything about time;

Time is of the essence, and time is the trick.
Funny, it was seven years ago
I borrowed that five dollars from the Company's funds.
I intended to put it right back;
It was easy to get away with, hard to put back.
Once on the books I could not adjust for it.
That was the beginning of my system.
I remember how innocent it all seemed then
And I was drunk with my secret vision.
With the Company growing, so big and sound,
And I controlling the books to the last penny,
I developed a system that worked, a real tap root.
First I drew on a bank in Birmingham.
It always takes a few days for the mails.
To cover that check I would draw on a bank
In Omaha; to cover that, on a bank in Scranton.
If I needed more time, on a bank in New York
or Boston. With business mounting to the millions
I always had a flock of checks in transit.
Of course they all paid off in time.
The auditors went through the books each year,
Found nothing amiss; they believed in money in transit.
I had it in a delectable state of transit,
Going around in accord with my stratagems
Which were figured with meticulous attention.
If it had not been for that first five dollars
I do not believe I would have done such scheming.
As it is, I have found it as easy to take
Twenty thousand dollars as two hundred
And nobody in the world knows the difference.
I have the figures in my head over the years,
It has been seven years now since I began.
I have kept my secret inviolable.
Inviolable from wife and family, or from any man.
The figure stands at over a million dollars.
I, Hurricane Ransome, am the man.
Everything pays off, everybody is prosperous,
The system itself is as strict and mechanical
As the whole process of making money is.
I am bound upon the wheel of my own design
And force myself into frenzies of activity
In presenting to the world The Visionary Farms.
I am absolutely bound by my own system,

Cannot even take a vacation of a week,
I must be on hand all the time, relentlessly
Fixing the books, covering the checks,
Bedazzled by my big embezzlement.
I have to keep a light shining in the world,
A fierceness of action and of energies
For the frenzies of the darkness in my heart.
As an actor I will not wince, or show a sign
Of the abysmal knowledge fighting in my vitals.
My wife, my child, Mr. Parker, Adam Fahnstock,
How could I do it? How could I betray you?
It is the evil getting me from the inside.
The slightest, innocent-seeming insinuation
When it all began, back in 1914,
Has grown in my hand to my most monstrous sin.
I am bound upon a wheel of fire.
There is no end to the agony I am in.

SCENE VII

SCENE: *Fahnstock's living Room, six months later. It is
evening.*

VINE

William, you sit over there. Suzanne,
Come and cuddle up by me on the divan.
We are going to hear Peter say his speech,
We will rehearse him for the Declamatory Contest;
Miss Williams chose the title, "The Turk Must Go."
Do you think you have learned it by now, Peter?

PETER

I have put a lot of time on it. I think
I can say most of it. Just think, maybe
I will get to go to the State Oratorical Contest.

WILLIAM

I was never good at learning speeches;
Mathematics is much more interesting.
Pete said some of it at the Duo meeting.
Our rivals, the IRT's, have orators too.
They are going to try to win the contest.

PETER

Duodecim is much better than the IRT's,
We have the best literary society
In high school.

Suzanne

What about the Happy Workers?

Vine

Suzanne, you were certainly energetic and fine
To form the little group of girls your age
And be the leader of the Happy Workers.

Suzanne

Well, Pete, why don't you say your speech?

William

O, Mother, did Pete tell you he has been elected
To be editor of the next year's Annual?

Vine

Yes, I think it is wonderful. And that you
Are going to be the captain of the football team.

William

Fullback. Pete is going to play right halfback.
It looks like we are going to have a heavy team.
If we work together maybe we can beat St. Paul.

Vine

Now let us listen. Go ahead, Peter.

Peter

Mother,
I really do not want to say it yet.
Give me a few more days to learn it by heart.
I need to say it to myself up in my room.

Vine

Well, all right, Pete, if you do not wish to.
We will rehearse it some other time, you and I.
Suzanne, you go up and get ready for bed.
I'll come and tuck you in, and give you a kiss.
Boys, you had better go to your rooms and study.
You children are all so fine, I love you so much.
(The children go out)
Ever since Peter made that wild left-end run
In the Creston game last fall, hurtling across the sideline,
And knocked me down hard to the ground,
I have had a pain in my chest where his head hit me.

Wendy

Pain is something that I cannot endure;
In it the intellect must abrogate
And give over to the brute, destructive forces.
Nothing could be more tragical than this,
That the mother, who saw her son in pride

As the hero of the field, should by him fall;
That he, her lusty image, a youth bold and swift,
Should knock her down on the way to a touchdown,
And all unwittingly be her instrument of doom.

GRAYCE

Something sinister broods over these avid scenes,
Something I do not dare to think about.
I, who think I drink from the cup of reality,
Who hope for hectic music and for headier wine,
Fascinated by the mere obvious excess of life,
Fret not only restive, but fare afraid.
Or if not afraid, troubled by the evidence.

SCENE VIII

SCENE: *Mr. Parker's living room, six months later.*

PARKER

Come in, Adam. It is nice to see you today.

FAHNSTOCK

Roger, things are getting worse. Vine is suffering
Much pain, and has to have hypodermics
Every few hours.

PARKER

        I am sorry to hear it.
I had thought the trip to Chicago would help.

FAHNSTOCK

We took her in a private car, and then
She underwent the highest voltage treatment.
Before that, you recall we had a machine brought here
On the advice of both the doctors.

PARKER

They are known to be the best in the world.

FAHNSTOCK

They could not diagnose her case for months.
It looked like pleurisy. Then they told me,
Secretly, that it is carcinoma of the lung.
There is no hope. We have not told Vine.

PARKER

Adam, if there is anything I can do for you at all
I will do it. To think of our close circle of twenty years
Being broken, and that Vine has to suffer so.
I will do anything in the world I can for you.

ADAM

William is going up to the University,
Peter is going to stay home and help take care of his mother,
I am trying to be strong, to see it through.

PARKER

Let me know if there is anything that I can do.
(Adam goes out)

BERYL

Through the young streets of the talking town
Awareness grows, as in ancient times and places.

WENDY

Ted has come back from the East to work for his father.

GRAYCE

Handsome and light, he wore a golden key ring
When he left. The doors are open to him, returning.

SCENE IX

SCENE: *Bub Woodward's Barber Shop. There are three chairs.
Ted Parker comes in, now out of college and in the business.*

TED

Hi, Bub, give me the works.

BUB

Okay, Ted.
We'll give you better than you got back East.

TED

Have you seen the new roadster I have just bought?
It is a specially built convertible, will do seventy.

BUB

No, maybe you will give me a spin in it some day?
How would you like your hair done, Ted, the same?

TED

The same. Don't cut it off too short, though.

BUB

You know me. I've got some new slickum to put on.

TED

Give me the works.
(Bub starts working on Ted)

BUB

How do you like being
In business? Isn't it kind of hard to settle down?

TED

I like it fine. It takes some time to nose around,

Learn the works, look into all the systems.
I have got plenty of ideas of my own.

BUB

Did you go out to the opening of the new dance hall?

TED

I drove out in the new speedster. We are certainly booming.
Ransome drew about sixty thousand for the opening.

BUB

Quite a guy, Hurry. Since you have been away at school
He has built that place up like nobody's business.
Did you see the head of the flock he got from Java?

TED

Of course, I have seen everything. It seems to work.
It seems rather crazy to call them The Visionary Farms.

BUB

Ted, it's not too bad. Since you were a little kid
Look how we have grown. Really not bad.
Your father was a true visionary,
Ted, when he began the works, and Adam Fahnstock,
Who spread the word to the ends of the country.
The town has boomed. I began with one chair.
I think Hurricane hit on a pretty good title.

TED

Well let me out of here, Bub. I've got
A date to take Molly Catherwood for a spin.

BUB

All right, Ted. There you are. All right?
Come in again.

TED

                    Sure will, Bub. So long. See you again. . . .

BERYL

What is the use of going so fast after all?
Is it a brave new world with six new cylinders?

WENDY

Fate has placed Ted in a fortunate position.
He may go as far as he likes. Who can stop him?

GRAYCE

Bub boasts that he has grown, but he has stood still.
Maybe he is the wisest one of all, the spectator.
Change and growth swirl around him: he stands still.
He is the true chorus to the actual scene.

Wendy
>He'll trim them often and keep them looking spruce,
>Paradoxical spectator! He'd never be a trimmer.

Grayce
>He'll keep his head in silence, observing the headstrong.
>They come to him to look better than they are.

SCENE X

SCENE: *The president's office at the Parker Corporation.*
Roger Parker is standing by his huge desk. Ted Parker is
talking to him. Roger Parker presses a buzzer. Adam Fahn-
stock comes in.

Parker
>This is very serious.

Fahnstock
>>What is the matter?

Parker
>>>>>>>>Adam, Ted
>Has found something irregular in the books.
>He has been looking into our various systems,
>As you know. Ted, show Adam the papers.
>*(He shows Adam a check and some bank papers)*

Ted
>This looks very irregular to me.
>As a matter of fact, it looks like embezzlement.
>Where is this money to be accounted for?
>You see, this one does not check off. I am
>Suspicious. I have studied the matter for several days.

Adam
>It certainly looks out of the ordinary.
>Our books have been audited by Smith and Smith,
>There has never been the lightest thing amiss.
>Roger, I suggest we call in Ransome.

Parker
>That is just what I am going to do.
>*(He rings a buzzer. Hurricane Ransome enters, at ease)*

Ransome
>Well, gentlemen, what can I do for you?

Parker
>*(Taking the papers from Ted and Adam)*
>Hurricane, this is a very serious matter.
>Do you see these figures here? And these statements?

They do not agree. It looks like the Company is short.
How do you account for these discrepancies?
*(Hurry takes out a 3x5 pad of paper from his left pocket. He
takes a pencil from his vest pocket. With meticulous care,
and seemingly without emotion, he writes down a figure on
the pad, looks at it intently, and hands it precisely to Mr.
Parker)*

PARKER *(Reading)*
One million, one hundred and eighty seven thousand dollars.
Hurricane, what does this mean? What is this figure?

RANSOME
I have embezzled precisely that amount of money
From the Company during the past eight years.
(They are all dumbfounded)

PARKER
Hurry, you couldn't do this to the Company!
It is unbelievable. It is incredible.

FAHNSTOCK
Good Heavens, Hurry, how could you do such a thing to me?

TED
I got suspicious when I saw these papers.

RANSOME
Gentlemen, I just got careless. I just forgot.
I forgot to cover the check I had in transit.
I thought I had an unbreakable system.
It makes me feel better to make you my confession.
Do what you will. I am washed up. Eight years.
Bring in the books, and call in the auditors;
I will show you precisely how I rigged it.

PARKER
Where is our reputation for honesty now?
Why this will ruin us all.

FAHNSTOCK
                              Think of our good name,
Our sterling reputation.

TED
                              I thought there was something
Phony about The Visionary Farms.

PARKER
Ransome, we will have to call the police.

RANSOME
Of course.

PARKER

Ted, call Chief Decker.
(He rings the phone)

TED

Chief Decker? This is Theodore Parker. My father
Wishes you to come right over.
(He puts down the phone)

He'll be right over.

FAHNSTOCK

This is incredible. I cannot believe it.

PARKER

We have trusted you implicitly for twenty years,
Putting into your charge millions of dollars
Because of our faith in your honesty.

TED

This will change the history of the Company.

RANSOME

I just got started and I could not stop.
Back in 1914 I took five dollars.
I could not justify it on the books
So I thought of a way to cover the withdrawal.
It worked so well I did it again, then again.
After a while I found it just as easy
To take out twenty thousand as a few dollars.
That is why I never took a vacation.
*(Fahnstock and Parker look at each other dumbfoundedly. Chief
Thomas Decker comes in)*

PARKER

Thomas, you have seen much in your time.
I have to tell you the worst that has happened to us.
Ransome has embezzled over a million dollars
From the Company. You will have to lock him up.
(Chief Decker gives him a hostile look)

DECKER

Why, Hurry, I wouldn't believe it. Come along, Hurricane.
(He takes him out)
CONSULTING AUTHOR *(Addressing his wand)*
Over the entire, the young, the hectic town
I wave this instrument, projecting news
Shall hurtle down the years their massive import.

SCENE XI

SCENE: *Jacob Herzog's furniture store. Jacob and his daughter
     Frieda.*

JACOB

I am one of the two Jews in this town.
Frieda, it is a long way back to Russia.
You have grown up to be a good girl
Under the aegis of our real democracy.
I am glad that you are on the Debating Team
With Levering Banfield and Peter Fahnstock.
Our store has grown big since you were little,
Since your mother died. I have been honest,
Have won the loyalty of many customers.
Who would believe what happened to Hurry Ransome?
He was always doing people good,
Speeding things up, enlarging the horizons,
Making more work, and urging strenuous efforts.

FRIEDA

He was so serious in Sunday School.
He always preached to us on good and evil.
He exhorted us to do good, to shun evil.
I remember the dramatic experiment he made
With a silver dollar, the pure one, the black one.

JACOB

Yes, who would believe what happened to Hurricane?
The people serenaded him in the County Jail,
Some with guitars and banjos, boys with saxophones,
A voluntary crowd of a thousand townsmen
Came to pay their tribute to the Hurricane.
They raised sums, they tried to bail him out.
The magnitude was just too much to cope with.
They formed a committee of his admirers
Even before he was sentenced, to get him out
As soon as possible from the State Penitentiary.

FRIEDA

I think he was evil. They should put him away for life.

JACOB

You are young, Frieda. You do not understand life.
The thinnest line divides the false and true.
It might have happened to your father.

FRIEDA

                              No, Father,
Not you. You are as wise as the world. What did he get?

89

Jacob

> He was sentenced to fifteen years in the State Penitentiary.
> His name is broken, his honor is gone,
> His wife has died of the shock, and his son,
> What can become of his young, his tender son?
> Always be a good girl, Frieda.

Frieda

> Father, I will.

SCENE XII

SCENE: *The office of the president of the Parker Corporation.
Mr. Parker is sitting at his desk. He rings a buzzer.*

Parker

> Adam, the banks are threatening receivership.
> It is a question whether we will be able to carry on.
> I command you to turn in your stock to me at once.
> It is imperative to cover the deficit.
> I cannot cover it all. You own a major block.
> I have decided that you must turn it in.

Fahnstock

> Why, Roger, this is inconceivable,
> This will ruin me. Would you do such a thing?
> Do you understand what you are saying?
> The value of the stock is worth now practically nothing.
> You cannot do such a thing to me.
> The Chicago bankers have withheld receivership
> Under the stipulation that I execute
> And bring us out of this. You know that well.
> They place a most absolute faith in me.

Parker

> I own this Company, Adam. My word is law.
> You will find in footnote thirty-four
> Of the contract we signed twenty-one years ago
> The powers delegated to the President
> To call in stock whenever he deems necessary.

Fahnstock

> Roger, my wife is dying of cancer.

Parker

> Adam, you will turn in your stock by tomorrow noon.

Fahnstock

> Your conduct toward me is intolerable, despicable.
> I feel that Ted has put you up to this.

I am the man who has made this Company gigantic and
    famous.
We have worked together as a powerful team
Through the full years of our maturity.
You know that the bankers believe in me, not you.
You are saving your own face at the cost of mine.
You are making your right-hand man the scapegoat.
Roger, are you capable of such vile trickery?
Neither you nor I was to blame for Hurricane.
You hired him, promoted, believed in him,
I with you. We both trusted him implicitly.
Now that he has pulled the wool over our eyes
So that we have been blind for eight whole years,
You are not man enough to take the rap
Along with me, but you would ruin me.

Parker

You will turn in your stock by tomorrow noon.

Fahnstock

You would do this with my wife on her death-bed?

Parker

Money is stronger than life, Adam, much stronger.

Fahnstock

You are vile, treacherous, you are obscene.
Your would trample on every decency,
Every one of our thousands of acts of good will,
Every fine and just and generous act,
You would destroy the home and the family,
You would destroy me when I most need you
For the weak motive of saving your own face.
You put my powerful nature in a frenzy
Against the gross wrong you are accomplishing.
You make me mad and livid with rage.
You are crazy in the head, Roger, you are wrong.
(He makes to rush out)

Parker

One thing before you go, Adam Fahnstock.
You have been getting too big for your own boots
For quite a few years now, for quite a long time.
I own this Company. I am the President.
You cannot command me. I am the law.
(Fahnstock rushes out in powerful realization)

FAHNSTOCK

O, whatever gods there are, give me restraint!
Deliver me from the evil power of hate.

GRAYCE

I like the idea of violence, not its use.

WENDY

What if Hurricane had never been found out?
He is vital as part of the upsurge of America.
If he had kept on, only Death would have found him out.
A curious villain to be such a heady hero.

GRAYCE

It looks to me like unalterable justice.
When everything is wrong, every one is right.
They all pull down the house on their own heads.
I cannot see any way out of this,
Am criss-crossed in my violent sympathies.

WENDY

It would be better if Hurricane had not been caught,
Better if the vast machine had gone spinning on
Without any hint of the infernal ructions.
Better if time had dreamed on the land, no fierce
Beast raged destructively in the hearts of men.
O it would be better if life were literature,
Something to contemplate coolly in the study,
Piecing together the nice puzzles of the world,
Indifferent to honor's devastation,
In the remove of books lost to suffering.

GRAYCE

Blood was from ancient times a way out.

WENDY

What happens in the imagination is real;
What actually happens is strange and evocative,
A long complexity, edging toward a sort of order.

SCENE XIII

SCENE: *The apple orchard of Adam Fahnstock's estate.*

FAHNSTOCK

Suzanne, close the door of the car. Come over here.
*(They stand under an apple tree in full bloom; it is June, 1922,
    the whole orchard is in bloom)*
Children, I have brought you out here to the orchard
Because there are many things that I have to tell you.

I want to talk to you here in the orchard I planted,
Where we have had the Maypole every spring, so many
Picnics, and every fall the fragrant cider mill.
It is a special place we have loved, since you were small.
I want you to look me straight in the eyes, each of you.
I have taught you to be honest, straightforward and clean,
We have given you everything that love can give,
You have grown up to be industrious and fine.
Now you must steel your souls, for this is hard.
You have heard the story of Hurricane Ransome.
You know that Mr. Parker and I trusted him,
That we saw him as a competent bookkeeper
Many years ago, promoted him, and elected him
Years ago to be comptroller of the treasury.
For eight long years he has betrayed us,
As you know, taking money illegally,
Cunningly and viciously from the Company
Without either of us suspecting it,
So cleverly did he cover it all up.
I married your mother in 1898,
The finest woman whom I had ever known.
We came out here when the town was very small.
Here I began my progress in the business,
Our love was perfect, and here you all were born.
We have had a wonderful and loyal family.
Strong as I am, it is hard for me to go on.
I must tell you the truth, and I will tell it.
While you do not know all of my affairs
You know that I own a great deal of the stock,
Yet a considerable less than the controlling part.
Mr. Parker has seen fit to call this in,
Which means that I have to sell it to him
At practically nothing, at great devaluation,
So that my fortune of twenty years is gone.

PETER

Father, I have forty dollars in my savings account.
I want you to take it.

FAHNSTOCK

        Bless you, son, that wouldn't help.

WILLIAM

Father, I will quit college and go right to work.

FAHNSTOCK

Fine, William, but I hope you will not have to.

Suzanne

    I will do everything I can to help Mother.
    I will pick her some apple blossoms, now.

Fahnstock

                    Do that, darling.
    We will have to live in a different way.
    We will have to give up many possessions,
    We will have to stick very closely together.

William

    The Parkers are the best friends of our family.
    I do not understand it, it seems too cruel.

Fahnstock

    The world is a place of struggle. We have to meet it.
    Now come close to me here, all three of you children.
    I want to put my arms around you, and love you.
    This is the hardest thing to do in my life.
    Steel yourselves now, boys. Suzanne, come close.
    We have done everything we could for Mother
    Since her terrible illness began.
    You have all done everything you can.
    We are up against something beyond us.
    I have not been able to bear to tell her
    And now I must tell you, I must tell you the truth.
    Mother is worse, and has not a chance for life.
    (They all weep, restrained by Fahnstock)
    Now you children must try to be strong.
    While there is love there can be no death
    For we carry love with us to our own end.
    Love we carry in our memories.

Peter

    Do you think Mother knows?

Suzanne

                Mother is so beautiful,
    I love her with all my heart and soul.

Fahnstock

                       Children,
    I do not know. The doctors have advised us
    Not to tell her. But about two weeks ago
    Late at night she called me to her bedside.
    Her suffering was for the moment slightly lessened.
    She told me that she had loved none other,
    And of her love and devotion to you children.
    Then she said nothing, but looked me in the eyes.

We held our hands together a long time.
Then she quietly took off her wedding ring
And silently she gave it back to me.
Then the pains came, I had to give her more morphine.
*(Toward the end of his words he takes out the wedding ring and
    holds it up to them)*

SCENE XIV

SCENE: *Home of the Everymans.*

CONSULTING AUTHOR

    (Waves his wand)
Thank you, ladies and gentlemen, that is all.
We are going to leave the action at this point.
All of these gentlemen have become madmen,
Due to the enormity and gross enchantments
Of the times, astonishing products of America;
Each might soon be at the other's throat
And lay some bloody forms about our stage
Not unlike the old, gross days of Elizabeth.
Now let us enjoy what's done, and let's construe.
Let us keep vile actions off, and bring on thoughts
To estimate these matters to a standstill.
We are not going to have the usual climax;
Originality is to leave it to your imaginations.
Homer is more realistic than Shakespeare.
You continue beyond the high peaks to the lowlands.
Violent actions are flattened out by the years.

ROBIN

You pay a tribute to the time's confusions.
We confess our lethargy and inability
To conclude the action dramatically.
Do we not owe fidelity to action?

CONSULTING AUTHOR

No, we owe fidelity to talk.
It is the temper of our times to rage
And talk tragedy into comedy.
Now Adam Fahnstock could kill Mr. Parker,
But all these men were too intelligent,
The matters too complex, too thoroughly understood
In one way, yet not understood in others,
As, that Ransome did not estimate himself,
The compulsive vessel of universal evil,
Yet understood well the actions of the world.

Adam we see in a Homeric rage
Who could heap coals of fire on adversaries,
Yet we contend he was too pure a man
To venture murder. Ransome will not break jail
And shoot the town up in a Western riot.
You know his character is such that soon,
The model prisoner in prison, soon
They will have him keeping the penitentiary books,
A true-to-life pure comic touch, is it not?

ROBIN

He's much too smart for fifteen years in jail.
By good behavior, that irony and mockery,
They will let him out in seven years or eight,
A halfway measure suiting our society.
Parker, the man of the letter of the law,
We may assume will feel no guilt, but go
In due time to his sixty-two-foot tomb,
The largest in the local cemetery,
Unblamed, the dauntless American Millionaire.
Or if guilt stung him, he would never show it.

CONSULTING AUTHOR

And Adam, by being too good would not be downed
But change his life and live in militant ability.
The Greeks would show one of his enraged sons
With purpose growing like a power in his vitals
Who, twenty years later in a red rage,
So pure and implacable a lover of justice,
The elders dead, would kill the son of Parker.

GRAYCE

I would like to see you work that out.
I would like a just action, less that's theoretical.
I wouldn't mind seeing some accurate shooting.

CHARLIE

I keep the emotional feeling of the conflict.
It is the new play to indicate, not overstate.

WENDY

Just a little like my Spanish folklore.

BERYL

Life's complex enough. Who'd think to tie it up
Into a neat dramatic package? Life is cloudy.

CONSULTING AUTHOR

I will put my wand back in my jesting pocket.
We see that everyman's both good and evil,

None knows quite the world, all are vexed
By impenetrable clouds of various fortune,
Caught upon the stage of time, mankind showing.
Some lights we turn up in our cynic syllables
To show the faltering steps of Everyman.

JASON

Attitude is all.

ROBIN

Ours is disinterest.
We have shown the brutal spectacle of the world,
Evading the true awe of reality,
To plumb down into blood-deep savagery,
But we would throw out scenes of the passional
And weave around them pleasing ideation,
Evoke, and leave the rest to contemplation.
Thus, in our modernistic, small society
Handle chaos, and keep a balance of sanity.

BERYL

Let us end it then on a round of drinks.
(She passes drinks around)
I propose a toast—

JASON

To purity of discourse.

WENDY

To the larger vantage in the smaller scope.
In times of hurtling egomania
A little touch of modesty is nice.

GRAYCE

To poetry.

CHARLIE

To dialectical maturity.

BERYL

Let us sum it up and drink to Comedy,
A bobbing freight upon a fashioned sea.

ROBIN

Disinterested, yet with some love of man.
There is a justice beyond character that is time.

SCENE XV

AUTHOR (Coming in abruptly)
I am the author breaking in here,
My name is Richard Eberhart.

I object to the limitations of the theater.
The whole of life cannot be contained in art.
This play is supposed to be true and real,
Yet the true reality is somehow lost.
There is more to human drama than all this fiddle.
If you feel the conflict of the characters
It is due to veils of artistry.
My passions were thoroughly aroused by Ransome,
Who brought Greek dignity to a town in Minnesota
By proving the ancient duplicity of man,
Reducing Parker from the possibility of a hero
And showing Fahnstock ruined by his own virtue.
I rather object to this show. My deep feelings,
Deep as the abysmal midnight of the stars,
Do not make arrow to your target seats
But fly a little wildly toward you there,
A sort of Northern Lights shaking your darkness.
So be it. I've had my say. Hail, and farewell!
My execution never mated my deep passions
And so I leave you with a semi-illusion,
A hint of greatness in a waste of folly.
The truth is somehow ever never found,
But is approximated. I bow out on approximation.
(He exits, bowing ceremoniously)

CONSULTING AUTHOR

How unceremonious of him to break in here!
Goodbye, old mystic. We hadn't thought to see you.
How should we need the author? The play's of everyman.
The plot has rolled up on us such momentum,
For all the author's carping about reality,
His titan hankering after the absolute truth,
That what we want is a further glimpse of Ransome.

ROBIN

Hear, hear. We demand it, and we must have it.
Can you conjure it?

CONSULTING AUTHOR

                    I still have my wand.
You will have noticed it is a simple pencil,
But symbolic, to write your imaginations.
My stealthy legerdemain is an ancient rite.
With this pencil I can write right and wrong.
I can right wrong. I can write right.
(General giggling)

Wendy *(laughing)*
>What a punning trickster! He's laming us.

Grayce
>I still hope there will be some accurate shooting.

Jason
>Attitudes may gall.

Charlie
>Another dialectic?

Robin
>We grow impatient. Hurry up with Hurricane.
>We want to know what happened to the Hurricane.

Consulting Author
>Attend—
>*(Blackout on this scene—Lights up on)*
>SCENE: *The Warden's office of the State Penitentiary. The
>Warden is sitting at his desk.*

The Warden
>I am the Warden of a great penitentiary.
>I have been at this business for a long time
>But I really don't know whether I'm coming or going.
>I might as well confess it. Nothing but factions!
>I might as well be trying to run the State Department.
>This morning a delegation came and castigated me
>For spending too much money on the prisoners.
>They told me I am not brutal enough.
>More prisoners should spend more time in the hole.
>They think we are getting too soft here.
>Yesterday a delegation came urging psychiatry,
>Wanting to set up a psychiatric clinic
>With daily treatment for each prisoner.
>There's politics on every side. The scene shifts
>With every change within the legislature.
>Either we're a torture chamber, or we're easy.
>I am imprisoned here as much as any.
>There is only one man in the whole lot I trust,
>He has been trustworthy for a long time,
>That's number 1525. I'll call him in.
>*(He rings a buzzer. Ransome appears)*
>Ransome, you've given me more ideas in eight years
>Than all the books I ever read on penology.
>I don't get time to read the books any more.
>I'd like to change seats, and use your cell

Where I could ponder the ways of man to man
In solitude, and find some true solutions.

RANSOME

Thanks, sir, I wouldn't change for a million.
There is too much to do! We're making real strides!
I wish I could hurry it up. What opportunities!

THE WARDEN

You've already helped me save thousands a month
On the kitchens. You've cut down time of preparation,
Improved the type of service and the quality.
I must say, though, we've never had so much chicken.

RANSOME

You penologists are all dreamers.
You have got to find something to interest them.

THE WARDEN

Since you have taken over the penitentiary books
They have never been out even a cent.
Just between you and me, Ransome, I need your help.
Will you help me with my income tax?

RANSOME

Just let me have it, I'll fix it up in a day.

THE WARDEN

All right. *(He hands blanks to him).*
                    Just keep it under cover, though.
You were always so full of big ideas,
Can you think of some new way to improve this place?
The men are restive. I want to avoid a riot.

RANSOME

Can't you see they are tired of making license plates,
Those horrible gray kimonos for the insane asylum,
Those eternal bedroom slippers for the poor house?
O yes, our baseball team is good, and football,
They love to kick the ball around at soccer,
To vent their spleen. That's good. And ping pong
Attests agility, and keeps them sane.

THE WARDEN

I agree, those ideas of yours were good.

RANSOME

The rockpile only satisfies their grewsome muscles.
They are tired of making big ones into little ones.
It doesn't satisfy their minds, their souls.

THE WARDEN
  Don't, don't talk too loud about their souls.

RANSOME
    Here's what I want. I want it done at once.
    It will keep them going half a year.
    We'll sell the results at profit for Christmas presents.
    We'll get each prisoner to paint a picture
    Four feet by three feet about a farm.
    I insist on quick-drying pigment for this deal.
    We'll have each paste his picture onto plywood
    And make a picture-puzzle of two hundred pieces,
    Half to be cut in the shapes of farm animals,
    And I'd prefer the likeness of some roosters.
    We'll say to the public, you buy your puzzle
    And take your chances. See if you can guess
    Who made it. It may be by a murderer,
    A forger, a rapist, or a perjurer.

THE WARDEN
    That will certainly while the hours away.

RANSOME
    If they won't sell we'll give them to the hospitals.
    Every prisoner has some creative desire.
    They are no different than those on the outside.
    (There is a knock on the door)

THE WARDEN
    Come in.
    *(Enter, The Warden's Secretary. He hands The Warden an
        envelope. The Warden opens it)*
                Well, Hurricane, what do you think of this?

RANSOME
    I think only to improve the institution.

THE WARDEN
    Your parole has come through! Here it is!
    I've worked hard to get it for you. Here it is!
    You have discharged your duty to society,
    May pack up your things and leave at once.

RANSOME
    Don't you know I know a good thing when I see it?
    I wouldn't leave here for a million dollars.
    Something has gotten into me on the inside.
    It is an absolute sense of security.
    No end to improvements. Why, Hell's bells, this is a cinch.

THE WARDEN

Ransome, what I'd really like to do
Is to turn my job over to you.
You could run this place the best of any.
If I can fix it, how about taking my job?

RANSOME

I have too many ideas on how to improve
The place. I want to work with the men.
There are more ways than one of boring from within.
I wouldn't take it for more than a million dollars.
(Quick Curtain)

ROBIN

Some say he was found in northern Minnesota
In a small woods town as a small bartender.
There twenty years later his old days were a myth.

CHARLIE

Some say he went to California and made a fortune.

JASON

Nobody knows what became of the Hurricane.

ROBIN

He seems to have become a myth of the society
That forged him real and brassy as itself.

CONSULTING AUTHOR

All in that town recognized in him their evil.
They thrust him from the general memory like sin.
They wanted to forget; they wanted to lose him
In forgetful years that would redeem them all.
It was a universal fault of that society,
Each partook of a remarkable error.
Time dreams on the land now. We savor a memory.
(Beryl passes drinks around. They all raise glasses)

BERYL

To the hero of an ardent situation.

ROBIN

What's past is what may happen any time.
There is a truth beyond character that is time.

(Curtain)

Devils and Angels

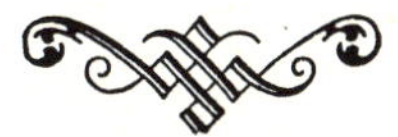

Devils and Angels

CHARACTERS: *Author; John, his son; Author's Wife; Robin Everyman; Beryl Everyman, his Wife; Devil; Angel; Professor I, Professor II, Member of the Audience, Sweetheart, Consulting Author, Mr. Sly, Mrs. Sly, Mr. Byfield, Mr. Masters, Baby.*

SCENE: *Office of the Author.*

AUTHOR

It is my originality
To stand and tell you that I am original.
I am a philosopher and a showman,
A man upon whom ideas have impinged
As impressions of the world have hit his senses,
Who between the sensory data and the ideational
Clatter, bemused, transfixed, and fascinated,
Has seen himself a clown of time, a clown
Of passage, a lightsome, lissome jester
Trying to make light of experience,
Testing reality—I can pinch my arm—,
An apparent solid mass in a massive flux
Of time, chance, incident, and possibility.
(Pause)
Whew! that was a long one. In all seriousness,
I have won my life by losing it.
I am going to try to show the truth,
In a certain way, about events,
Where character, which ought to be apparent,
Is not yet sufficiently emergent;
Where involvement may lead to the rim of ruin,
The ruin of love that is the involvement,
Because of an ancient purity of malice,
Or evil, or the Devil, whatever blasts the heath
Of heady adventure. It is the confounding force
Beyond the apparent harmony of character

That is the Hell-mouth devil of the underbrush,
The wicked smile lurking on the marble statuary.
Do I grow too fast? It is as simple as this.
A rich character ranges in his richness.
Rich characters act in love of life,
They think they control the situation,
But they are controlled. In these chancy times
It is important who is at the controls.

(*Pause*)

See this theatre? See the world?
See the lovers love, love take a tumble?
I am your man who is at the controls.
I will show you the conflict behind the scenes.
The controlling force is a trick as old as the earth.
It is simply to tell the truth. Are you ready?
(*A child bursts in, about six years old*)

JOHN

Dad, bring home the bacon.

AUTHOR

           Go away, John,
I'm making a speech. Reality is always
Breaking in upon the meditations of art.

JOHN

Mummy wants you to come home. Sister
Has got a stomach ache.

AUTHOR

           Go along, John.
Wives always want one to come home. You'll see.
They do not appreciate the forensic taste of the world.
There is always a bellyache somewhere.
There is always something wrong, the world's bellyache.
You go home. Put on your space helmet.

JOHN

           All right, Dad,
I'm blasting off, so long.

AUTHOR

         I'll bring home the bacon.
I'll be home after I have mastered the world.
Eventually everyone goes underground.
(*Author's wife dashes in keyed up, right*)

WIFE

You come right home. The baby's awfully sick.
I think they call it projectile vomiting.

I'm scared. Come home right quick and help.
I left her with Grandma. Come at once, I need you.

AUTHOR
Okay. What's the hurry? Do not forget
She represents the future. We are her past,
She is shoving us off. Projectile vomiting!
What a symbol. She is pronouncing upon the whole affair
Of life. She protests life and parents.

WIFE
Never mind, break it up; come, I need you, now.
(Wife exits)

AUTHOR
Reality is always breaking in on us.
I thought I was telling the truth about reality.
But projectile vomiting! My own very little baby
Has got a sort of loud-speaking system of her own.
The little tyke must hold her local stage.
How provident that life has grandmothers.
Between a mother and a grandmother they should do.
Now back to the serious business of—did
I say art?
(Enter, Robin Everyman and Beryl Everyman, his wife)
Greetings. I was muttering to myself about art.

ROBIN
We were just straying in here hand in hand.

BERYL
We feel more in love now than when we were married.

AUTHOR
Love gets better as time goes on. Indubitably.
Isn't this about your tenth? A good beginning.

ROBIN
We were dreaming of the chance that made us meet.

BERYL
I couldn't have found a better man than Robin.

AUTHOR
Love gets better, everybody knows that. Use
Perfects it. A paradox hangs in it though:
It also gets worse. It is not what it used to be.
You take the rigors of the tensions for granted.

BERYL
We're the downright mated pair.

ROBIN
                              Not up in the air.

AUTHOR

It takes an act of imagination to find the truth.
Comedy is a defense of the intellect.

BERYL

A little intellect goes a long way with me.

ROBIN

She has a woman's basic sense of the central.

AUTHOR

How can we resurrect the giddy compulsions
That drove us to the frenzied heights of youth?

ROBIN

Tomorrow and today are better than yesteryears.

BERYL

We have living faith, not killing fear.

AUTHOR

How would you two like to act in a play?
I'd make you great lovers, in a literary way.

ROBIN

Sure thing. Have you a part I could do?

BERYL

Why, why not? Wouldn't I make a good siren?

AUTHOR

Everybody is somebody else. Let imagination draw
You in new characters, gaudy, young, believing,
The central actors of a vexed romance.
I'll put you through high, histrionic paces,
Daring to recreate the madcap past.

ROBIN

Okay, we'll do it. Inform us. Good-bye, now.

AUTHOR

Be ready for the opening in one month.
I'll cast some other characters, if need be.
I'll interpose my own objective reality
As a commentator, sometimes, maybe. Good-bye.
(They exit)
The sufferings of lovers well up before me.
*(Enter, unexpectedly, swiftly and slyly, the Devil, dressed in
    customary black, tail and all, carrying a long, traditional
    three-pronged fork)*
Great God! Do my eyes deceive me?

DEVIL

They do not. I am not a king of deception.
I am the master of intellectual clarity.

AUTHOR

You have found me out. My conscience! Spooks!
I thought you didn't exist. Have at you!
*(The Author rushes at the Devil, engaging him in a wrestling
bout. They struggle furiously, falling to the floor and rolling
over and over as one gains and gets atop the other, then the
other does the same)*
I've got you! Down with you! I'll hit you on the head.
That it should come to this! Wrestling with the Devil!
(The Devil throws him over, gets on top)

DEVIL

The Hell with you. I've got you down, I'll quell you.
It is necessary that you be purged. I am purgation.
I've been waiting for this. I'll kick you in the groin.
*(The Devil is on top. The Author eludes his grip, and gets on
top of the Devil. They pant and struggle)*

AUTHOR

What do you think this is, a sexual bout?
I can't help laughing while I'm fighting.
*(Author laughs hysterically. The Author is still on top. He is
tiring the Devil)*

DEVIL

What the Hell, you're an arrant Calvinist.

AUTHOR

Had enough? Get up then, and be decent.
*(The Devil gets up. They stand up ruffled, perspiring, trying to
assume their dignities. They stand apart a few feet, when the
Devil pulls out a knife, lunges at the Author like a football
tackler, throws him violently down, holding the knife over his
head. Author exclaims, chokingly)*
You Devil! Damn you! You are too subtle.
Don't you know the Marquis of Queensberry rules?

DEVIL *(Poising the knife)*

I'll be the death of you if you don't do as I say.

AUTHOR

Say on. What do you want? Is this reality?

DEVIL

I'll mutton you. I'll cut you up in pieces.
I'll make you stew in your own immoral juices.

Can't you see that I love you? You must love me!
Why did you jump me?

DEVIL... *wait*

AUTHOR

Let me up, I'll talk.
*(The Devil releases his victim. This time they separate and take
  seats apart, facing each other, toning down)*
Animal necessity, I guess. What should we talk about?

DEVIL

Your arrogance almost cost you your life.
You cannot live without me. My love of mankind
Is deep-seated, ineradicable, and absolute.
When I find a member of your tribe
Who thinks he is the master of the intellect
I appear, and trounce him with cold clarity.
I am really an angel in disguise.
Without me you would not know reality.
You would be a pallid, insignificant creature
And never know true creativity.
Learn to love me and you will be truly human.

AUTHOR

What makes you think that I couldn't kill you?

DEVIL

I am subtler and swifter, I know all your motives.

AUTHOR

I admit I didn't think you really existed.
I thought you were some sort of mental illusion.

DEVIL

Do you have a drink?

AUTHOR

Help yourself, there's whiskey.

DEVIL

Have one too?

AUTHOR

Surely, or do you want blood?

DEVIL

Whiskey is a good substitute; quite soothing.
(They drink)
Make sure in your dealings with reality
That I am involved in the creative process,
Will menace you in every adventure
If you offend against my primal selfhood.
I am your very ancient companion.
I'll bring you back to earth. Don't stray far,

Or leap to heavenly disjunctions,
For I am in the heart of what you are.

AUTHOR

Now you are talking like a gentleman.
I'll remember you are always behind the scenes,
Liable to pop out like a maniac.
I'll try to love your hated physiognomy.
That's the fascination of the difficult.
I'll let you have your way, as recommended.
You are both destroyer and preserver,
A paradox, and my ironical visitor.

DEVIL

You have to love me. Hate and love are much the same.
You loved me when you were wrestling fiercest.

AUTHOR

That sounds like something out of a book.

DEVIL

Keep your books, they are innocent enough.
Just do not forget, in the meshes of deep action,
I'm always there, your subtle lover, to help you
In your thrashing mind, to see the truth.

AUTHOR

This is a very deep paradox.

DEVIL

                                        Laugh
If you like. You may have the whimsical.
I hope I have taught you a good lesson.
I'll sink back beyond your mind now.
(The Devil goes off stage, stealthily)

AUTHOR

Good night. Say, what goes on here?
Is this the truth? Do I wake, or dream?
(Wife enters)

WIFE

I thought I told you to come home. You look
Ruffled. What is the matter? The baby's crying.

AUTHOR

I have just had a bout with the Devil.

WIFE

I told you not to drink alone. It is disgusting.

Author

This was a real Devil, believe it or not.
We have been wrestling on this very floor.

Wife

Come along, dear. You were always too imaginative.
But I love you for it. You always had
A startled look.

Author

Your hopeless visionary.

(They exit.)
(Author steps back on stage into room)
In the scuffle I must have lost my wallet.
(An Angel appears from the left, a traditional Angel all in
white, with long white wings, a neuter creature of light)
I say, do my eyes deceive me?

Angel

They may.

Author

You have the appearance of an angelic host.
I never thought I would confront an actual angel.
Am I the insufferable guest of the next world?

Angel

I appear only to those who do not think they need me

Author

You have an aura. You are lovely. You soothe
My animal nature and make this scene undramatic.

Angel

I am beyond good and evil. I am the enlightenment.
I dwell in the intuitions of poets and visionaries.

Author

You startle me into an unearthly realization.
I see that you do not mean to take any action.
You are an eternal idea. Do you know, Angel,
In this room I recently wrestled with the Devil?
I am having a rather full day of it.
I should not have expected it. Are you viable?

Angel

You earthlings are always using dictionary terms.

Author

Just a moment. I have to speak to my wife.
(Author goes off stage, reappears quickly)
I told her I would be along presently.

How did you get down to the United States?
I think of you by way of ancient, early Greece
Back to the land of the scriptures!

ANGEL

                      I understand you.

AUTHOR

I thought you dwelt only in a world of light,
In the impossible heaven we all believe and deny.

ANGEL

I am pure spirit. You have often dreamed of me.

AUTHOR

You have the charm of the evanescent. I see
That you are the presentation of a mystery;
That nothing could be more excitable or unreal
Than that on the same day I fought with the Devil
I should be startled by an Angel, with real wings.
I see that our association is subtle, unbelievable.
You make my heart heavy that you are not dramatic.
I object to you there all in white, radiant,
With your unearthly pallor, your total engagement;
You draw me out much against my will;
Your loveliness is too extravagant, you chill
My membranes with remembrance of much suffering,
And I am almost afraid to look at you.
What are you doing here, an absolute
Come to unnerve me in an august illusion
Beyond the powerful acclamation of my blood?
Why, I fought with the Devil on this floor,
And after that I had honest discourse with him.
You, there, white and radiant, so near and so far,
I do not feel any kind of intercourse with you.
An other-worldly chill pervades your look,
See, I want to do the talking when you are here,
I am afraid of you; I am composed of good and evil,
I cannot escape the bonds of my human nature,
In fact, I do not wish to escape my humanity;
I am dismayed to see you, a vision; frankly terrified.

ANGEL

There, take it easy. I am supreme intelligence,
Albeit other-worldly. You have a measure of intelligence,
Else you would not be troubled and furtive.
I come to bring you harmony and serenity,
To remind you of a height beyond your condition.

I have come like a blinding of the insight,
Those times you have had in the night without words,
Or in the day beyond care; those inner reaches
Of your spirit, when you dreamed beyond death;
Those hours of meditation on a mountain,
Those endless moments of perception in daydream;
Those apparently unreal and disjointed times
When you felt the world as an immaculate radiance
In the hand of God; in those incredible intuitions
I was always there, beneficent and without harm to you.

AUTHOR

You are too pure; you make nothing happen.
I cannot confess to you my total sinfulness
And knowledge of evil. You elevate me to a dream
Beyond the necessities of every day,
And beyond the necessities of every man and woman.
I want to show the drama of earthly life,
Tragic and comic, good and evil, life and death.
No doubt you are part of my essential suffering.
No doubt there is a meaning in your coming here,
Although I cannot see it. Do you want a drink?

ANGEL

Thanks, I drink only the nectar of the gods.

AUTHOR

All I have to offer is some straight Kentucky bourbon.

ANGEL

If you came to me I would show you wisdom
But if you were wise you would not be so interesting
And if you were angelic you would be too intelligent.
I have appeared to you only for one reason,
To suggest that you hold everything in suspension,
Be not a painful dogmatic absolutist,
Be most yourself while trying to overcome it;
Be not lost in consciousness, in awareness of evil,
Nor be consumed in rosaries of the ineffable.
Know only that I exist in intuition,
As I am vital here to you in my kindly light,
That there are mysteries beyond the despairing mind,
And truths beyond the rational intellect.
I am going to walk out of this room now
As if I had been a dream in a white time.
Do not think that an Angel is also an illusion.
(Angel glides off stage, right)

AUTHOR

This is about the strangest thing I have seen.
At least I could grapple with the Devil. This Angel
Worries me with some excellence far beyond me.
My wife. My wife! She will think I am going crazy,
Seeing visions here in the room of every day.
(The Angel returns, holding a hand aloft, saying)

ANGEL

You were meant to be your best self, not your worst.
You were meant to know the efficacy of prayer.
You were meant to search the boundless reaches
Of humility receding ever to new depths,
Leaping ever to new heights of realization.
You were meant to know, in the meshes of the flesh,
The sublime unapproachability of the spiritual!
You were meant to know man's essential yearning
Toward that which is beyond man, unspeakable.
(The Angel glides off stage)

AUTHOR

Now I've had it. Now I have confronted myself.
What I need is a long drink.
(He takes a drink)

                         I remember one time
When I went to the Chinese theatre
In San Francisco. I listened to the drama there,
Enthralled for hours by words I did not know,
Lifted and carried on the musical syllables,
Seeing the masked actors moving to and fro,
Suspended in a beautiful dream of consciousness,
Enchanted with the music of the instruments,
As if some drama of high and rare import
Were dreaming deep significance; at last
I left, and asked an English-speaking Chinese
The import of the play. He said casually,
"A comedy about a city whore"
And dashed my dreams of heavenly discourse,
Of tragic pity, our Western suppositions,
To another dimension of sophistication,
Leaving me shaking leaving the little theatre.
(Wife bursts in)

WIFE

I will not have you there going on drinking.
Come back home and take care of your baby.

AUTHOR

Okay. I want to say something to the audience.
Do you mind if I say something to the audience?

WIFE

Make it quick. I am filled with anxiety—

AUTHOR

You go right on. I will follow shortly.
American man is always following the woman—

WIFE

Certain things are a matter of necessity.
(Wife departs)

AUTHOR

Before I make any heavy pronouncement
I should like to make a serious announcement,
To speak for the freedom of the individual—
*(The scene changes abruptly. There rush in members of a
    tableau, two Professors, stylized)*

PROF. I

Why did he not get to be,
To be,—the head of the English Department?

PROF. II

Why should he want to be,
To be,—the head of the English Department?

PROF. I

It is plain for all to see,
To see, why it could not be.

PROF. II

Why could it then, not be?

PROF. I

His wife told the wife of the head—
Can you imagine what she said?

PROF. II

I cannot imagine what it could be,
Could be. What could it be, could be?

PROF. I

His wife told the wife of the head,—
She might as well be good and dead—

PROF. II

What, what, what did his wife say?

PROF. I

His wife said, it was only yesterday
That the wife of the head, the wife of the head—

Prof. II

I'm sure she is already good as dead.

Prof. I

His wife said that the wife of the head
Had a coat of rabbit, not lapin!

Prof. II

Not lapin? She said rabbit instead?

Prof. I

She said rabbit, and not lapin,
That's what caused all the laughing.

Prof. II

What a serious indiscretion.
Oh, No! Not this! Not rabbit!

Prof. I

She did not know enough to say lapin!
And so her husband is not the head
Of the English Department!

Prof. II

Not the head of the English Department?
O Rabbit! O Robots! Oh lapin!
(The tableau departs, instantly)

Author

Apparently the truth hangs on wires of thin—
Who am I communicating with? Oh you!
*(He beckons to a member of the audience. A member of the
audience comes up on stage)*

M. A.

I suppose you are Mr. Everyman, the tops?
I do not know what you are talking about.

Author

Oh, yes you do. You know more than I do
About it.

M. A.

About what?

Author

About the play.

M. A.

I have been waiting for the play to begin. I paid hard cash for
seats to get in.

Author

Are you alone?

M. A.

I have my sweetheart down there.

Author

    Nobody is ever alone, not the audience,
    They come to be dispossessed of loneliness.
    If they only knew that their essential
    Loneliness was their most lordly possession.

M. A.

    I do not like this kind of talk. Say, you,
    I did not pay to hear the author talk.

Author

    Who did you think was doing the talking?

M. A.

    I did not think of it. I brought my girl to the show.

Author

    I have arranged for a crackling spectacle.

M. A.

    You are trying to placate me, you are.

Author

    Of course I am trying to placate you, I am,
    It is my desire to make you happy.

M. A.

    Happy, what do you mean?

Author

                              I mean happiness.

M. A.

    Happiness is out of the question, Bud.

Author

    Don't call me Bud. I'm the originator.

M. A.

    Okay, what have you got to offer?

Author

    What have I got to offer? A coffer.
    It is a coffer I have got to offer.

M. A.

    It sounds like a coffin. Is a coffer
    Something that you ought to offer?

Author

    Better than a coffin. You can proffer
    The casual offer of a coffer,
    You can do it without any other bother,
    It is like a spiritual mother.

M. A.

    How can a coffer be a mother?

Author

    It is more central than a brother,
    Being on a plane with a father.
    The mother-coffer is like a smother
    Of all the riches of the earth, rather.

M. A.

    I think you are going beyond me.
    Your rhythms are affecting me.
    I feel a strange, compelling glee,
    As if I were going to break into poetry.

Author

    Hocus-pocus, mystery in banality.
    I hope you do not mind a little levity.
    I have wrestled with the Devil, actually,
    Been confronted by an Angel, materially,
    Want you to know yourself the lucky taker
    Of the riches, the method of a maker
    Come down to earth, an Everyman
    Who lives within the love of man
    And does not have to see Devils and Angels.
    I, as Author, plan to be your evangel.
    (His sweetheart comes nervously on stage from the audience)

Sweetheart

    You have got me in a terrible dither.
    I have come to take him back to his seat.

Author

    Welcome on board. You are going to sail him hither?

M. A.

    I am just beginning to enjoy the show,
    Feel as if I were going on a limitless voyage.

Sweetheart

    You come along now, don't wait a minute.

M. A.

    Don't mind her, Author. She is really a baby.

Author

    She will take you on a real voyage, maybe.
    (Sweetheart takes Member of the Audience by the hand, exit)
    Women are always coming to take us away
    To reality.

M. A. (From audience)

                    And just when I was getting gay.

Author

    I think I will come down to the audience too.

Truth, they say, is all in the point of view.
(Enter, Wife)

WIFE

The baby is better, you do not need to come now.

AUTHOR

No, I won't. Well, that is an idea for later.

WIFE

Mother got her to sleep with a lullaby
She used to sing to me.

AUTHOR

Lucky little baby,
If you only knew how well off you were in your cradle,
Before the heaviness of experience began.
(There is a knock at the door. Enter, Consulting Author)
Why, hello, Detector. Glad to see you, come in.

C. A.

I thought I would take a bit of tender time
And wrap it around you; I feel close to you.
My life has become a bibliographical extravagance.
I have got to the six hundredth item on the Old Boy.

WIFE

May you get to the end of the book, but may you
Never come to the end of understanding.
So glad to see you.

AUTHOR

Won't you sit down? There.

C. A.

Have you come to any conclusions yet?

AUTHOR

We never come to any conclusions at all.
We are pure continua. Not so, darling?

WIFE

I let Robin think he is getting precisely nowhere.
He loves indecision. I have learned to play the game.

AUTHOR

It would be awful to feel that we had arrived.
Success is the kiss of death. I want to keep struggling,
I want to hug the years of bitter struggle, the vision,
I do not want to lose them, or to lose it.
It is only by daring to throw oneself away
That we find and clasp our souls.

WIFE

That is all right,

Just so you do not throw away *me*. You have the dream,
But I have you in reality. Don't ever not humor me.

C. A.

We all have more hold than in the old days.

Author

I have an arcane problem I would broach.

C. A.

You are moving into life's complexities?
Life's old complexities again? The fault?

Author

I seek immersion that will bring solution.

C. A.

Time has baptized you with knowledge already;
Your well is full. It flows over at the lip;
We all drink your words. You are the man.

Author

That is kind of you, cozy to have old friends
Think well of one. You always were a flatterer,
A twinkle in your eye from the Lakes of Killarney.
In all seriousness, I want your advice.

C. A.

I am uncomfortable at thrusts of reality.
Reality for me smells of the lamp and the study.
If one can keep his own house in order
One should not be put to theatrical tortures.
However, as they say, play on, play on.

Author

Reality is black and white, fictions are fey.

Wife

He can never see it the other way.
The truth is something beyond our sight.
I vote it is never either black or white.
*(Enter Mr. Sly, Mrs. Sly, Mr. Byfield, Mr. Masters. Mr. Sly
    is a short, psychotic man of sixty, a famous composer. Mrs.
    Sly, ten years his junior, has the overblown look of a weathered
    actress. Mr. Byfield, an old friend of Sly, and a casual
    friend of Mr. Masters, is a sixty-year-old lawyer. Mr.
    Masters is a composer, about forty five, who is self-sufficient
    and even-tempered.*
*The scene is high-pitched, immediately hysterical, fast moving,
    and vicious.*
Mrs. Sly takes a decanter of gin, pours out three stiff drinks one

*after the other and pours them, so to speak, down the throat of
Mr. Sly, who drains them off quickly. She takes two shots
then herself. She offers a drink to Mr. Masters. They are
sitting down. Mr. Sly rises, thrashing around the room as
the scene may be played)*

MRS. SLY

Take a drink, Masters.

MASTERS

Thanks, I will take one.

MRS. SLY

Have a drink, Mr. Byfield.

BYFIELD

No, thanks, not for me.

MRS. SLY

Take another drink, Masters.

MASTERS

No more, thanks.

MR. SLY *(Viciously)*

Now about that official job at the White House,
Masters, composer to the President,
I'm going to have this out with you right now.
I am going to do everything in my power
To keep you from getting that job, do you hear?
(Mrs. Sly moves in seconding his attack)

MRS. SLY

Why did you have to write to the Secretary?
Don't you know that my husband is in command?

MASTERS

You told me I had been officially elected
By the White House Board of Governors of Composers,
An honorary job for which I did not apply.
You sent the Secretary to see me at my house,
Who notified me of my official election
As your successor. What are you talking about?

MR. SLY *(Feeling the drinks, growing shrill, fierce)*

I am going to see that you do not get that job!

BYFIELD *(Alarmed)*

This is all nonsense. You have been friends.
You ought to get together. This is all nonsense.

MRS. SLY *(Attacking)*

What right did you have to write to the Secretary?

MASTERS *(Who remains throughout in self-possession)*

I have done nothing wrong. I did not seek

The job. I do not belong to the Board of Governors.
When the Secretary informed me of my election
I naturally wrote to him to ask him a few questions.

Mr. Sly

You shouldn't have written to him to ask questions.
I am the authority. I am in the Chair,
I am in power. You will never get that job!

Masters

I was told that I had been duly elected
By the honorable gentlemen in the Government.

Mr. Sly

You went behind my back.

Masters

                              You're talking crazy.
I did nothing of the kind, I did nothing wrong.
You must be afraid of me. I am innocent.
You look right now like a demented animal.

Byfield

There, there, calm down, this is all nonsense.
You have been friends, you ought to get together.

Mr. Sly

I will do everything in my power to keep you out!

Masters

You are drunk. You look hideous. You are crazy.
I am appalled to see you sunk in bestiality.

Mr. Sly

I never forget. You have offended my sensibilities,
You went behind my back, you wrote to the Secretary.
I am the master here, I am in power.

Mrs. Sly

You shouldn't have done it, Masters, you shouldn't
Have done it.

Masters

                    I have done nothing wrong.
You offered me a high honor in Washington
To which I was duly elected. Now you are mad,
And raving. I am walking out of here now.
If there is justice, I would like to know where it is.
(*Masters rises, goes to exit, followed by Mr. Sly who rushes in a
    frenzy after him, shouting as he departs*)

Mr. Sly

Don't you tell the President! Don't you

Tell the President. He'll put you in your place,
He'll put you in your place. Don't you—
MASTERS *(Leaving)*
So you have got the President fixed, too?
So you think you have, sad Machiavelli?
(Curtain down on the scene just shown)
C. A.

Why, this is the real old dogfight of mankind!
How did you think up such an improbable situation?
WIFE

The whole thing seems too hysterical to be true.
AUTHOR

The truth is more theatrical than the theater.
C. A.

The scene lacks an essential dignity.
You have reduced a man in high place to a beast.
Why do you have to show a frenzy of drunkenness?
Would it not be more devastating if sober?
AUTHOR

The truth is the truth and that is all there is to it.
This man had malice, the coldest malice aforethought.
WIFE

I thought Mrs. Sly was an old meany.
Imagine thrusting all those drinks down his gullet.
C. A.

It is justified because of the frenzy and madness
Of the times; it is a spectacle of unreason.
How would you carry it on?
AUTHOR

The way it would go.
In the official report of the yearly meeting
When Masters was elected by the Board of Governors,
Sly expunged the notice of his election from the record.
WIFE

You mean he took it out? Why, that is baseness itself.
The other members were there at the election.
What did they do? Did they do nothing about it?
AUTHOR

He probably told them a sufficient number of lies
So that he held the whip handle over them
And beat them into line by malice and cunning.
They knew all, and they did nothing about it.

WIFE

What insufferable pride!

C. A.

One-man rule!
This is very near to one-man rule.
An example of what has become of our society.
I can see that Mr. Masters had no recourse.

AUTHOR

He was pure, he was innocent, he had none.
You do not fight back for gentlemanly honor.
You either have it or you do not have it.

WIFE

It is hard to see the truth smashed to bits
And the evil-doers win in worldly ways.

C. A.

Nobody is entirely good, or entirely evil.

AUTHOR

Don't be soft. You have no idea of the coldness,
The implacable nature of malice and hatred.

C. A.

You have given us a terrible look at reality.
But things like this have happened every day
From Cain and Abel. You kept off bloodshed anyway!

AUTHOR

We have got to fight harder for our freedoms,
Some way.

WIFE

The way is not to resist evil.
Evil repaid by evil is never any good.

C. A.

You are moving to ideas of the sublime
Which are the hardest ideas to entertain.
They seem sometimes so far from reality,
Yet who could deny their inevitability?

WIFE

Christ said to turn the other cheek.

AUTHOR

Ah, yes, that is a profound, endless mystery.

C. A.

I must depart back to bibliography.

WIFE

Come to see us again, another time.

C. A.
        I shall.
AUTHOR
                Don't forget to ponder life's dark looks
        When you are looking up the facts of lives in books.
        How was Masters supposed to know the snake in Sly?
        He did not know it. He thought he was an Angel
        Come to do him good.
WIFE
                                O double irony
        That he was a Devil, to do him harm.
AUTHOR
        It is one thing if it were only personal.
        It is another thing when it is national.
C. A.
        It all comes down to a matter of temperament.
AUTHOR
        Whenever you see the rage of tyrant power
        You know there is insecurity at the core.
C. A.
        The truth is in the ego. If not all of it,
        Much of it is there. The old man's ego
        Was wracked with jealousy of his successor,
        Evil jealousy of the younger elected one.
        He wanted the blind devotion of a son.
        He took a petty and a small revenge
        On him for being good, just for being decent.
        He therefore took the stance of wrathful Jehovah.
        It has something to do with loving the Devil.
        This whole matter is not to be ravelled out,
        Maybe, but is an instance of rooted complexity
        Dark as man. Extended, it is the warfare of nations.
AUTHOR
        I perceive this. The Devil came to me.
        We wrestled. We almost killed each other.
        From the violence of this symbolic dream
        I learned how much the Devil wanted love.
        It is not in the nature of things, but Masters
        Might have given him love despite injustice.
WIFE
        Don't condone his awful wickedness.
C. A.
        He did not know that he wanted love.

(The Devil bursts in, wheeling a baby carriage in which is a
two-year-old baby. The Devil is in Devil's garb, but dandified)

AUTHOR

Why, my bloody antagonist. This is the Devil!
What are you doing here?

DEVIL

                                   I am engaging the future.

BABY *(Wails)*

Waldo, Waldo—

DEVIL

Down with the past! Down with the present! I stand
Brimful hale to control the future.

WIFE

                                          What effrontery!

DEVIL

You people are as boring as Hell. Your discourse
Is as tedious as the long days of the Inferno.
I am going to bring this baby up right.

BABY *(Wails)*

Waldo, Waldo—

DEVIL

                                     I am an absolute Pope
For control. I snatched this child from Heaven,
That pale station without merriment or action.
I am going to teach him how to wield power.

WIFE

What an absurd medievalist you are.
I will get him a bottle of milk, warm and kind.
(Wife has just addressed child in last line, but)

DEVIL

Who, me?
(Wife gives denying look)

AUTHOR

He needs the milk of human kindness.

C. A.

Surely, Devil, he can do without your deviltry.

BABY *(Wails)*

Waldo, Waldo—

WIFE

                              He cries out for the Over-Soul.

AUTHOR

He already objects to the human condition.

C. A.

> How philosophic. He wants to go back to the womb,
> Luxe, calme et volupte. He dissents already
> From the primal Devil-handling of the baby carriage.

DEVIL

> You mortals talk like school children. You will never
> Unravel me. I am firm-knit in impressionable Nature.
> I infiltrate the Psyche. I alarm your reason
> And must say again that your arguments are boring.
> Your will toward justice without me in the scales
> Is the joke of the ages.

BABY (*Wails*)
> Waldo, Waldo—

WIFE

> Dear Satan,
> Cannot you perceive that you are scaring the child?

AUTHOR

> I suppose that right now we are looking at the very **truth**,
> A confused spectacle without adequate resolution.

DEVIL

> At least that is a grown-up remark. Your absurd play
> About trying to find out the truth of human affairs
> Fills me with glee. You lack the Devil's subtlety.
> (*At this point in walks the Angel, all in white, radiant, re-
> splendent, and serene*)

ANGEL

> Do you mind if I have the last word? I am the spirit.
> Do not give all to the Devil. Remember me.
> I announce the ineffable quality of the good.
> Satan, you have tried all of your tricks before.
> You are unregenerate. You have never tried prayer.
> (*The Angel walks over to the baby carriage, lifts up the baby,
> and fondles it like a mother*)

BABY

> Mamma—Mamma—

ANGEL

> I will take care of this child forevermore.

AUTHOR

> We seem to be controlled by Devils and Angels.

C. A.

Devils and Angels control all of human power.
*(Black out on the Author, the Consulting Author, and the
Wife. Spotlight on the Angel holding the child, the dandified
Devil looking on. The Angel holds the baby as a mother,
while the Devil makes a static, imploring gesture with his
hands, as if like a Father, wanting the baby to come to him.
This dualistic pose is held as the spotlight slowly fades)*

(Curtain)

The Mad Musician

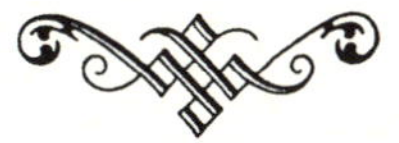

The Mad Musician

CHARACTERS: *Robin Everyman, formerly the Author;
Beryl Everyman, his wife; Jason Curley, a scholar, formerly
the Consulting Author; Wendy Curley, his wife; Charles
Westgate, a teacher, also a poet; Grayce Westgate, his wife.*

SCENE: *The house of the Everymans. An evening in the
autumn of 1950.*

(The Curleys and the Westgates enter)

ROBIN

Welcome, come in, it is nice to see you.
I hope you are all prepared for the revolution.

JASON

Don't tell me you are going to be revolting?

WENDY

Jason has been diffident about your plans.

GRAYCE

We've heard about it too, and are all ears.

CHARLIE

We had the usual sitter problem, but here we are.

BERYL

I put Peter to bed early: hope it works.
I read him an extra story, about Barbar,
The Elephant. He seems to like large animals.
Robin, will you get the drinks?

ROBIN

                    Of course.
How about bourbon and water as proper libation
To open our theatrical celebration?
(Sounds of assent)

GRAYCE

Robin, I'll take beer if you have some.
(Robin exits to get drinks)

BERYL *(To the Curleys)*

Have you got a house yet?

WENDY

                        We're still looking.
We have one in mind on Standish Street.

BERYL

I heard of one on Prentiss Street the other day.
You probably want to be farther out.

JASON

                             I think so.
We don't have to move unless we find just what we want.

BERYL

You must have forgotten about it in Paris this summer.

WENDY

I'm afraid we did. It was nice to be rootless.

CHARLIE

And *we* have to sit in our three rooms, brooding.
Maybe next year I'll get an assistant professorship.
We feel being edged out, with Tom and Priscilla.
And need some playing space.
(Re-enter Robin)

ROBIN

                         Here we are.
(Passes around drinks. All take seats. The men get together,
*   talking, take out cigarettes, etc. The girls go into a momentary*
*   huddle, talking)*

GRAYCE

The most remarkable thing has just occurred.
Wait till I tell you. You wouldn't believe it.

BERYL

A new scandal among the graduates?

GRAYCE

                        No, worse.
It involves an eight-year-old girl and a five-
Year-old boy. Mrs. Cafavis told me about it
Yesterday.

WENDY

              She is the wife of the Greek professor,
Isn't she?

GRAYCE

            Yes. It's terrible if it weren't so funny.

BERYL

What happened?

Grayce

                            These kids have been playing together.
Margaret already seems to be quite neurotic.
With another or two they've taken to taking
Their clothes off, and showing themselves. Well, yesterday
Margaret played an awful trick on Timothy,
Who's only five. She wrote his whole name, in ink,
On his penis.
(They all laugh)
                 His mother was so ashamed and angry
She scrubbed and scrubbed, and practically wore
Poor Timothy's skin off.

Wendy

                               She is the wife
Of the psychiatrist?

Grayce

                 Yes, she's unphilosophic:
And her husband doesn't know what to do about it.

Beryl

We ought to do something about that sort of
Thing at once. I admit it is pretty funny.
(They chuckle, joining the men, who have not heard the con-
versation. Enter three young men students in their middle or
late twenties, whose education was interrupted by the war
and who wish to become actors. And three young women in
their early twenties, aspiring to be actresses)

Robin

Come in, ladies and gentlemen. I hope you have had
Fine summers. It is very good to see you again
And awfully good of you to do this for us.
Have you all got your lines by Garrick rote?
(General assent)

Robin *(To the others)*
Our friends have submitted generously to a work-out
And are going to hold the mirror up to us
From what we've set them in our nervy lines.
This is our revolution against the public
Theater, debased to calculations most of money.
We'll have it in our house, and we'll oppose
Intellectual freedom to commercialized convention,
Here, where every idea of the imagination
Can have its sway, no subjects will be barred,
And poetry may reach its full sonority,

That's if we're capable. Thus with humility
We work, and try some simples of invention,
Some trials of our fortunes with the Muses,
For all the large designs we have in mind.

JASON

What did you come on, after our discussions?

ROBIN

But wait. We also make a little revolution
Against the little theaters, which tend to make
Impossible actors into improbable actors.
Nothing like trying to do the impossible.

BERYL

Robin, don't apologize. Let's get started.

ROBIN

We are interested in Everyman
And shall attempt, in various dimensions
Various struggles, passions, and predicaments.

JASON

I am prepared to uncase my imagination.

ROBIN

There'll not be much respecting scenery.
A chair, a table, the simplest accoutrements.
Our next small room shall be the seething stage,
A little 'O' to represent the pent-up world,
A certain restraint to let imagination go.

WENDY

I think it sounds like fun. What costumes?

ROBIN

Of the plainest. And not much make-up. A certain
Bareness.

CHARLIE

          We're waiting. Could you brief us on the action?

ROBIN

The first abstracts some instances of struggle
In a young, passionate, revolutionary man.
It is some glimpses of the rebel ego.
The Son is the protagonist, opposed
To Father, Mother, and Psychiatrists.
I'll take the part of the protagonist myself
Out of a certain diabolic streak
For, frankly, he is another self of mine,
And of yourselves, a part of Everyman.
(They all sit back, new drinks are served by Beryl. The ap-

*pearance of the actors is in the following order: Son, Father,
Mother, Schoolmaster, College Psychiatrist, Professional Psychiatrist, Choruses, Joseph, Arthur.
The young actors sit in the main room, exit to right and reappear
as required in the further room, the inner stage. Sometimes
they return to the main room, giving a feeling of informality)*

Inner Scene I

(The play beginning, Robin as Son)

SON *(In soliloquy)*
Beethoven is my pleasure and my pain
As I sit in a mist of inconsequence
In this low house where I would burst my brain
Entangled as it is in these immensities.
Music is my art, music is my soul,
The flight of structure my all night coffeeless distention
Here where nothing is real, but everything seems,
And wearing sounds in my head like clothes in tatters
I do not know yet what is a comely appearance,
For harmony is to me as far as Naragansett,
And I fear they have me of reremice sense,
These cold, cynical professors of the King's English,
These unbloods of no compendious experience,
These grovellers to the scholar's desiccated wish;
Their talk a footnote, spineless vigilance.
O the Latin the flat, the Greek the light and high,
What good did all that do me? What to me
Now the preposterous rigors, the rank, spiritless rules
Of that washed old school where none was free?
What was the use of that asylum of affront,
A mental hegemony of regimentation,
Where against the pricks I caught my death
Of it, but won some spiritual visitation;
Visitation that now I sit with all night long,
Which is the secret springs of my order and disorder,
The draft and depth of my soul's impossible desire
To fight for the truth, whether in glory or sordor.
I hear them talking—
(The baby begins to cry upstairs)
      I hear him crying, instead.
Reality is never pure. Beryl, go and do the honors.
Sorry, we'll have to wait a bit. On the
So-called "real" stage there would be the problem

Of making his cries convincing. I've never heard
A stage baby's cry that wasn't phony.
JASON

This begins on a heavy note. A real old rant.
A thought you were going to mill a Comedy.
ROBIN

I guess it depends on the definitions.
BERYL *(Returning)*

He wanted a glass of water. We have a game
And ritual every night I forgot.
He takes a big sip, and I take
A big sip, and he takes a little sip,
And I take a little sip;
A big sip, a little sip,
A little sip, a big sip,
And finally, clutching his fetish blanket
He goes off to sleep. I hope it'll keep.
JASON

The waters of life.
ROBIN

                                        Have another drink?
(Beryl pours drinks as desired.)
ROBIN

I'll take a line or two, to restore the tone.
The draft and depth of my soul's impossible desire
To fight for the truth, whether in glory or sordor.
I hear them talking—
*(The Father and Mother come in, sit facing Son, who says
     nothing. The effect is as of a tableau)*
FATHER

You must not use any more money this week.
MOTHER

You must not see Miss Savage any more at all.
FATHER

You must fit yourself to make a living.
MOTHER

You must come to dinner in a black tie on Sunday.
FATHER

You must become more practical; indeed,
You must think only of the law, of the family honor,
The old house on Puritan Street, and what we have been.
MOTHER

Give up that wretched girl. You must!

She is beneath you, not even in the register,
From the West, and her family is unthinkable.

FATHER

If you don't do what I say I'll cut you off.
If you don't do what I say I'll cut you off today.

MOTHER

You must give her up, we are not of that kind.
You must do what I say, you must mind me.
(The Father and Mother exit. The Son sits silently, thinking.
  Enter, Schoolmaster. He addresses the Son)

SCHOOLMASTER

I understand your difficulties. My sympathies
Fly to your marrow, but the world is a hard structure.
I have seen your ponderous disposition mired
In the slough of febrile, unrealistic junctures,
I have watched you somewhat like a hawk, and seen
The basic failure breeding in your bones,
Behind your eyes the stark, revolutionary gleam,
On your hands the knots of work, in your throat groans.
I have believed in you, have given you my belief,
Have ranged along your mountainous eccentricities
With patience come from youth-observances,
Full of doubt; one must observe the amenities;
I am for you but I am also against you;
The cost is too great, the prize you seek too high.
The world is rough. Torn too, I give my advice:
Keep your feet on the ground, renounce the sky.
(The Schoolmaster exits, left. The Son continues silent, medi-
  tating. He then gets up with a shrug, leaves the inner stage,
  joins the main group, and watches what follows on the inner
  stage. Enter, College Psychiatrist and Dean. The Dean
  says nothing, listens)

COLLEGE PSYCHIATRIST

Now that the door is closed, Dean Longhead,
I can tell you of the discovery I have made.
I have discovered that our patient eats his toenails:
It is my opinion that the young man is mad.
He has appeared to me rude, vain, cruel, gloomy;
His ego is self-defeating evidence of spleen;
He is unsocial, and talks with bitter, cryptic wit.
Furthermore, I must point out that he is unclean.
We must watch him carefully and test him
With the new psychological measurements I have;

If he scores low, as I am confident he must,
His presence among us would not be safe, but grave.
*(The Dean keeps silent, as if meditating, nods a kind of assent,
     as if being put upon; both exit. Professional Psychiatrist
     enters the inner stage. The Mother enters)*

PROFESSIONAL PSYCHIATRIST

I know how terribly wrought up you are today.
I have studied the dossier I have of your son.
Of the many sources I have tapped in this case
Your own lengthy confessionals are as a truncheon
With which to beat him into line, and to beat you,
Madam, if I may say so, into submission
Before my comprehension of your own situation,
Which seems to me of critical internal dimension.
I suggest you come to my office every Wednesday
And learn to do typewriting, possibly shorthand;
There is nothing so good and so relaxing;
Give up bridge, cocktails except when bland,
Try not to vex your friends, and at dinner
Never allow your son and his extraordinary friends
To talk of music or of musical conceptions
For, as we have seen, this always comes to bad ends.
I appreciate your candor in the formal dossier.
I understand that you did not wish to bear your son.
The whole thing was a mistake. And that your husband
Left for decades in China before his life was begun.
I also understand that you have a large income,
With a taste for expensive furniture, Tibetan treasures;
That, when he menaced you when he was in school
You went to the Mediterranean as a palliative measure.
I note here especially the trauma at his birth,
That he growled when young, with stance of an animal
Much too long, that as a little fellow he was vicious,
Delighted in sharp instruments, was like a cannibal
In being violently able to get his way;
That early he developed the solitary and lonely, the surly,
And that with the others he did not choose to play.
He refused you as nurse, and that was very early.
What's the latest?

MOTHER

                    It is this awful girl again.
It is the same thing as it was last year,
Only worse, for this one is an intellectual.

O how he tortures me! He mocks me every day!
He will not call up. Then the phone rings
After midnight, a falsetto voice nervously announcing
That they have run away and eloped, of all things!
Or again, even later, that at a party in Mayfair
They were locked in the cellar of a house on fire.
I called the police in each case. They reported back
No report, nothing amiss. Tricks of hoodlums and liars!

PROFESSIONAL PSYCHIATRIST

We were successful in avoiding the marriage last year.
After all, your son, having no means of support,
Is still in our power; we can do as we wish.
We are not yet, I think, at our last resort.
It is part of wisdom to be subtle, but forceful.
It is part of our job to be two-faced.
I am sensitive to your matrimonial debacle,
I am alert to his potential destructive malice.

MOTHER

I am so terribly afraid he will marry that girl!
The other one was at least an aristocrat,
At least a girl of the social whirl, although a creature
Of frail edge, who had twice been in an institution.

PROFESSIONAL PSYCHIATRIST

We weaned him away from her by power and fright.

MOTHER

This new one is always down at heel; what a sight—

PROFESSIONAL PSYCHIATRIST

I think your son is on the ragged edge
Of a very serious mental imbalance.
It is a medical fact that a certain too much
Will push a mind over the rational fence.

MOTHER

I am distracted almost beyond endurance.

PROFESSIONAL PSYCHIATRIST

Typewriting will soothe you and make you patient.

MOTHER

When he comes to dinner he will not speak to his father.

PROFESSIONAL PSYCHIATRIST

The case is dangerous, we must get him out of Harvard.

MOTHER

My husband and I will do what you say.
It is a trying situation; we are willing to pay.

PROFESSIONAL PSYCHIATRIST

    Good day, come again some other day,
    Come soon, call up my Chinese secretary;
    Meanwhile, I'll be quizzing Tom, Dick, and Harry
    To cut the ragged edges of this thickening history.
    (Exit both from inner stage)

Inner Scene II

(Son leaves the main room, enters the inner stage, speaks to the
    audience in soliloquy)

SON

    All my ebullience and reachy nature
    Unpistoned, and in a crank case. My flight
    That nature meant, or purposeful ambulation,
    Stopped before I have made any heady start,
    Stopped on the ground; on the grounds of what, I know not.
    My energies, sometimes succinct, nice, vivifying,
    Sometimes amorphous, massive, multiplying, or nullifying,
    Gone in the gross heap of somebody else's opinion.
    I am locked and stocked in thought, unable to move.
    I take long solace of Leonardo. Leonardo
    Knew the cold glint of actuality;
    With rational intellect I'll follow his science,
    To guard my turbulent essence. In me
    The great mutations of the world are acted;
    I am sick almost to doomsday with eclipse;
    In me they shall have a worth of remembrance.
    Gloom is the only comfort I can find
    And music the only well-heart of the world
    In the dark fastness and makeshift of my mind,
    Abysmal knowledge fighting in my bowels. O
    I was never good at football. Those leaden-calves
    Strike me as wasters of motion; those ball-chasers,
    Swilling advice, censure, and water between the halves,
    Look to me like comic characters;
    And those tepid spectators with insipid yells,
    Dressed for the occasion, their mothers in stunning furs,
    Mild fathers dreaming of their days on the track, or in shells,
    Seem like dogs on show, a race of thoroughbred curs,
    Ruffian man, dressed up in sporting clothes.
    The masters, dull everyone, without imagination,
    Calling virtue obeisance to precedented grooves,
    Hounded together in their impotent stations,

Who should be leaders, or rear those of the nation,
Cohere in their stultifying inferiority
To a species of well-meaning weaklings; whose ration
Was my bane; who did what they were told in entirety;
And drummed into my head with their evil drums
Their scared wisdom, their reliance upon fact, and fear
Of originality or the spirit of man; thinner faith
Propping another buttress to the church each year.
That was bad, but now it is worse, this life.
The shadows of my Puritanical ancestors
Come to me here in this room; their tricky light
Somewhat sportive among the purple bindings:
How can I be myself in their despite?
Away with the folly of their knowledge; policy
Eating the carcass of university society;
The past of their calamitous docility,
Their blood flowing like a stain through many minds.
I would I could break out. I am sick with identity.
Every composer haunts me from his page
And blazing in my mind with ceaseless magic
Smites me to the blindness and fury of rage,
Rage before the impossibility of fame
And fury before the impossibility of perfection,
My fury and my rage fruitless conquests
Of my own impotence and self-deception,
In which I know myself mean, low, worthless, ragged,
Calculating the clammy force of my self-pity,
Glossing the facts; embossing my ability;
Concealing fertility of a destructive wish,
In a cold climate where there is no violence;
For music can exalt the mind too much;
Has exalted mine; has made worthless the world
Where the finest sense and sensibility cannot touch;
Has changed the face of every man and woman,
Made earth a gloom to my idealism,
Destroyed the functions of usable connections,
Made revolution the size of realism,
And set me with its demon principle
To the farthest reaches of my mind and stature,
To the doing of all doing and undoing
In the depths, and in the cisterns of my nature.
(Exit, son)

Inner Scene III

*(Three months later. Christmas Day. Office of the Profes-
sional Psychiatrist. The psychiatrist is reading. Father and
Mother come in, agitated)*

MOTHER

I'm sorry to have to see you on this day.
Our Christmas Day has been spoiled. It is revolting!
I had to cancel the dinner we planned for ten persons.
I'm terribly upset. Yes, I'll have a glass of sherry.

PROFESSIONAL PSYCHIATRIST

Now, be calm. Maybe no great damage has been done.

FATHER

We're sorry to have to call you to the office today—

MOTHER

Last night our son called us on the telephone.
He wanted the car. We did not need it, and gave it.
At midnight the police called and said there'd been a crack-up
On the outskirts of Mayfair; she was hurt, and he was gone.

PROFESSIONAL PSYCHIATRIST

How did it happen?

FATHER

                              I have no doubt they were drinking.

MOTHER

I don't know how much longer I can stand it!
Our son ran from the scene. At least he was unhurt.
It seems in the wreck and wrack her face was smashed.
O, I hope this doesn't get into court.

PROFESSIONAL PSYCHIATRIST

                              I'll see to that.
What were the extent of the injuries?

MOTHER

                              A witness
Said her jaw was badly broken, and deep scars
Laced her face. How could he do such a thing?

FATHER

He doesn't even know how to manage a car.

PROFESSIONAL PSYCHIATRIST

Be calm, and don't worry. It might have been much worse.
He may have been stunned, not run away on purpose.

FATHER

He has locked himself in his reading room since then.
The authorities will only enter, if ordered, by force.

We have been patient with him for many years,
But the time may have come now to be fierce.

MOTHER

He is a minor; before the law we are to blame.

FATHER

I want you to put him into an institution
At once, before he may do something even worse.

PROFESSIONAL PSYCHIATRIST

You know, this is only a minor affront,
If you could see it that way. I have many cases;
You assume, under the heat of the moment, too much.
Let us treat this gently, and study it slowly.
Be patient. Let us take everything into account.
I'll let you know what I think we should do about it.

MOTHER

All right, Doctor. But this is much too much.

FATHER

You assure us with a common sense point of view.
Let us know when ready what we should do.
*(Exit, saying good-byes. Four actors appear, on inner stage,
    two men and two women; they speak alternately. The effect
    is formal, static, didactic, a kind of tableau)*

CHORUSES

CHORUS I

I'll speak about the father.
Fate it was to have a son more intellectual
Than you were when you went upon the sea.
A man of action has no great acclaim
Unless events conspire in actions great.
    You were a merchant shipman, you seemed free;
    You loved the ordinary, and you sent home money,
You trafficked with the world's unconscious freight;
But little thought you had a son to tame,
Confronted by his macabre quality,
Caught in his incalculable audacity.

CHORUS II

I'll speak about the mother.
Yours are the sins of vanity, selfishness, and pride.
You put yourself against the laws of nature.
You worshipped money and you escaped from duty,
You mistook a glittering tinsel for reality.

Neither in husband nor in son you found love,
It was always yourself you were thinking of.
Thinness of soul results from vanity;
How thin you look in your aspect cheerless and haughty,
How cranky, raw-boned, loveless is your stature,
Who for vanity to the simple things has died.

CHORUS III

I'll speak about the son.
The times have made your seriousness absurd,
And worked against you crass contamination,
They have conspired, and had with crippling tricks
Bent your nature to blasts of waste and woe.
        But deeper, and more far-reaching, fate had
        In the making to make you rich and sad.
Your dignity, not meant to be slammed so,
Built up a will to kick against the pricks.
And you were wiry to cry abomination,
You were wires to fetch and cage the soul.

CHORUS IV

And I'll speak about the Choruses.
From ancient language, tones sealed in time and death,
Your purposes are lost in modernity,
You lack the revelation and the caution,
Hybrid-pipes of doubtful prophecy.
        To the dismal nature of this spectacle
        You are the forced, ineffectual oracles.
Can nothing exhaust your powerful lethargy
Nor truth itself swiftly untwist this torsion
And strike a light through this enormity,
As of old, a salutary breath?

CHORUS I

The father thinks he is doing right, the mother
Feels she is doing right, the professional psychiatrist
Thinks he is doing right, and so does the son.
Each thinks the wrong inheres in the other.
Each in a sense is a self-hypnotist,
And even if they loved they would still be undone.

CHORUS II

Nobody is subtle enough, nobody sufficiently plain,
Nobody has courage enough, and nobody enough blame,
Nobody is eager enough, there is not enough time—
None disinterested—each has something to gain.

Each will go into the nothingness whence he came.
Fate has a plan, as a composer has a frame.

Chorus III

This man is full of mighty life. But deep
The chasms in his brains where Nature is.
He is her instrument to know herself,
Great mistress at whose feet men fall down.
He fumbles in his days with murky Fate,
His youth contorted with all ways to go,
He'll go them all. He knows not where to go
Or which to do, revolves them in his head.
To others loveless, his is a rich, deep love,
A forceful nature striking right and left,
All in shadow-mime within his room,
His fight absorbed in reading of the ancients;
The ancients with their great, heroic roles
Perplex him more, who, fed on literature,
Sees less clearly than if fed on facts.
Each way he looks a savage conflict lies,
None knows what most he wishes; none will help him;
Then plunging in the deeps of music theory
Where truth was thought to teach him how to act,
Confusions reach him; deeper, deeper reading
He is thrown out upon a myriad ideas,
Inflamed, unhealed; and worse with every master.
The stubborn head thinks truth resides in letters.
The ego is his sole authority:
When most alive, others he hurts then most.
And then the least he knows of this, or cares.

Chorus IV

He found no life to mate with his desires.
He thought that none could teach him anything.
Mercurial youth mints only the image of
The absolute; nothing else will boil;
Self-yeast of criticism leaps to others—
(*Turning to Robin*)
Robin, you're playing a trick on the audience.
You have left out the professional psychiatrist.
Does this mean that you approve of his actions?
But, wait; I will needle him myself.
If this is to be an original, lashing theater
I don't see why we can't clap the author out
And let the Chorus speak its mind itself.

I think the learned Doctor is corrupt,
A weedler, a mimic, a player off of sides,
A man without essential character,
A kind of lawyer balancing the niceties
And adding them up for a substantial fee.
He does not care for mankind, he has no love,
Using with skill his modern instrument
For self-advancement, in his cynic knowledge.
*(Robin does not answer the accusation, but leaves his chair,
moves swiftly out of the room, and enters the stage, left,
dressed as the Son, holding a Comic mask through which he
says, in an artificial kind of speech, mocking and taunting)*

SON

I put my finger on their hearts in halls
Of learning but pin to walls paper dolls.
They have their Ph.Ds, their books, their lectures,
The hollow men, the stuffed men, self breeders
Who lack all truth and find all kinds of slogans.
They live within their own enchanted circles
Patting each other's heads with sweet love-calls
As each his secrets to the others tells,
And the dull cannot tell false manufactures,
Leeches of poisonous purple of these bleeders;
But the virile see upon the walls all tokens
Of spiritual dearth and wastage of these dazed uncles.
Which should give light, a university, appalls,—
And nurse to every inspiration, and spells
Of insight, and goals, glares with cranky factions
Each teacher selfish where his trenchant reader
Would search and never have his spirit broken,
Would work if truth were hid amid the murk.
Most where they urge me on they irk me, falls
I take, a pompous antic kills and quells,
Absurdity creeps to the upper lattices,
Invectives hurl themselves like viable pleaders,
Faithless I walk where I was never woken
Among imponderables of their shirking shaking.

CHARLIE

I'd like to come up and say a stewing word.

ROBIN (SON)

Well, why not? We might as well break down the form.

CHARLIE *(Goes to inner stage)*

Here in a modern time of jibing chaos

This knotted animal, this freight of growth,
This ego hit between the eyes with love
From the mere look and propagation of the air,
This spirit in a world of worsening spirit
Is face to face with brazen violence,
His blood cut off from the roots, his blood dying,
His anger engendered and his whole force engaged
And we should hail him the modern man of wrath
Who in creative ecstasy is come
To purge the world and make us see again.
*(Goes off, goes back to his seat in main room. Robin goes off
    stage as Son. The Choruses sit on the stage, smoke, make
    soft, inaudible talk, as if part of the social gathering. Perhaps
    one or two wander out and sit with the others)*

JASON

Maybe you should be a composer yourself, Robin;
Your concepts are a kind of chamber music.
Lack of inevitability in the action
Although you supply the motive well enough,
Or hint, at least, at its corrosive grain,
Evoking the mental division that makes for frenzy,
Lack of inevitability in the action
Will keep it what it is, our parlor game.

WENDY

I liked listening to you, Robin, you were fine.

BERYL

I thought you all were. I'm eager for more.
(The baby begins to cry again)
Oh, Poor Peter, I'll go up again.
Nice of him this time, don't you think,
To cry just at a break.

GRAYCE

                         Give him a kiss for me.
It holds my attention, but it doesn't seem realistic.

CHARLIE

Maybe it has a touch of the universal.

JASON

On the contrary, I'd like to bring up a point.
Isn't it taken from real life? It seems to me
I recall some years ago some baleful antics
Of the sort. Is it true to life? If so,
Wouldn't you run into difficulties there, Robin,
At least of bad taste?

BERYL *(Returning)*

            He's asleep again.
  He seemed to be having a rather sinister dream.

CHARLIE

  My ignorance of music is profound.

ROBIN

  How do you write, if you don't take things from life?

JASON

  It is a measure of artistry to mask them,
  To manage by skill a cunning metamorphosis.
  Art is the hardest thing of all to make.
  It must be thoroughly plausible, yet be a trick
  So far withdrawn from life as to seem real.
  Isn't this too like the composer Pendleton?
  Too like his early life, his noted troubles?
  I've often cautioned you toward the impersonal.
  The ideal of Everyman precludes the use
  Of any man; of all possible real actions
  Those suited to the stage should not be personal.
  Abstractions should be made from myriad actions
  Which have a universal application
  Without affronting actual situations.

WENDY

  Aren't you being too theoretical, Jason?

ROBIN

  Something of the actions and the feelings
  Comes, I admit, from Pendleton. But years
  Have passed. The world now knows his music. Besides,
  If you'll permit of my outrageous vanity,
  The feelings are mine. I've done as best I can,
  To manage the piece as if I were the hero.
  If you should wish, and all here should agree,
  We could effect a fictional sleight-of-hand
  Without much difficulty, make the protagonist
  A poet or a painter, some other creator
  To mask the perturbing facts, and salve your consciences.

GRAYCE

  I shouldn't think it would be necessary.
  I always dreamed of the Romantic composers
  As wild men; for me, make him wild, and wilder.

CHARLIE

  The passing of time would make the problem inoffensive
  As I see it. Must we apologize for life?

Beryl

> Jason is usually correct, and always sensitive.
> I think you should remove the slightest implication;
> It is a wrong idea of composers anyway,
> More like what we know of poets or painters;
> Van Gogh, or Christopher Smart, or Holderlin.

Robin

> After we've finished let's see what you think.
> Shall we begin again? I am in for a long attack.
> *(Exit, reappears on stage as Son)*

Inner Scene IV

*(The Son, sitting in his study, begins to muse, walks and paces
about the stage, as he talks as if to himself, or stands still for
periods while soliloquizing)*

Son

> They think me mad, they think me queer, but they
> Are so. In me much straightness grows from a hard root.
> I play with them as upon a kind of toys
> To make them jingle; their every point is moot.
> The doctor with his silly strictures, that oaf
> So good to dupe; that man paid by the college
> To take my measure, why, I play him tricks,
> Him sundered readily in his ponderous knowledge;
> How could he have grown so old to know so little?
> One cannot respect the brains of these people.
> I balance him in his sessions to a tittle,
> Compounding my essence while he goes to sleep.
> My father I loathe, my mother I cannot endure.
> Each day I fight back into my savage youth
> As each day I would fight almost onto my bier.
> Weariness is the reward of the search for truth.
> The keepers of the English, locked in after thoughts,
> Each following another's pious instigations,
> None sensitive, none fertile, all in imitative tattle
> Incorporate their oppressive concatenations:
> Where is there one of them who loves music?
> Where is there one of them with originality?
> Where is there one with the potentiality
> To speak to and nourish me spiritually?
> O'er shady groves I hover. I must find,
> Where most it lives, in lucid contemplation,
> In lonely use, by the grappling hooks of the mind,

What all these fail to give me, elation.
The clerics as well, who served with lip service
Sure that they were comfortable, softly living,
The one who spread false joy, without experience,
Who would handle me thus sends me shivering
From the evil the religious do without humility,
The thick fearers of action, false preachers,
Contemptible. And that one loved to be my teacher.
But all is abuse. The world cracks from all these fakes.
Least likely, but stuffed in their rich poses
Are most of my contemporaries,
Sniffing collegiate honors through dirty noses,
Sure there is a plum in an editorship,
Certain of the glory of a fraternity club,
Addicted to debutante's coming out parties
Or harnessed in the glib gear of the snob;
Or feeble in the supposedly wicked brawl,
Purse-loose victims of their father's gall,
Successors, dress-well, to what slick successes,
Mother's darlings chancing the society ball.
I hate them all. I loathe and abominate them all.
Strength leaves me as my vision leads me up
To strident action; above and standing tall
Evil his good cup hands me, but I cringe to sup.
It must be done. In me Justice is riding.
In me now many fears are going or gone.
Night long, day long, my strength comes out of its hiding,
Justice in the solution. It must be done.
(Exit from inner stage. Joseph and Arthur, two graduate
      students, appear on the inner stage)

JOSEPH
      I suppose you have heard what happened lately. Have you?

ARTHUR
      I have mused upon it now some months.

JOSEPH
      I should think conscience would smite him to the core.

ARTHUR
      Strange is fate. He is better off than he was before.
      The subtle balance between reality and dream
      Was not upset. He exorcized his devils.

JOSEPH
      But for a certain obliqueness of the stroke,

And who can speak about premeditation
Conclusively, he would have killed his father.

ARTHUR

Had he killed him, the story would be different.
The absolute reality of the law
Would have closed in on him. The moral law
Admits a soothing element of time.
His father was shorter than he; I have often wondered
If he had struck the blow had he been taller.

JOSEPH

His mind was cold as steel and clear as crystal.

ARTHUR

It is good, however, that he did not have a pistol.

JOSEPH

His troubles are those of a whole civilization.
In his mind was not unity, but division,
Where should have been faith obtained derision,
Where warm-eyed faith, the calculator's precision.

ARTHUR

Do you think he will ever live it down?

JOSEPH

It is like an old story, in another town.
He was lucky. What happened in actuality
Was like the wishes that would make him free;
Enough unlike them not to make a Tragedy.

ARTHUR

To me it seems pretty life-like. Life goes on.
Homer is more realistic than Shakespeare.
You continue beyond the high peaks to the lowlands.
Violent actions are flattened out by the years.

JOSEPH

Put it down to youth; if you like to truth.
(They exit)

WENDY

Jason, what were they coming in for?

JASON

They are Choruses, explaining the action.

WENDY

Haven't we had enough of Choruses?
It's getting to be all Choruses and no action.

ROBIN

Wendy, I thought it might be more interesting

To have an oblique look, to report the action.
It varies the pattern. Do you think it sly?

GRAYCE

I'd rather have seen him do it.

ROBIN

                              He might have killed him.
Then what would I do? This is more philosophic,
And, furthermore, allows another scene or two.
We'll torture him on. We'll make a man of him,
His early hell-bent furies deracinating
And show the latest chorus sensible.
Well bred young men may sputter, fret and fume;
It is not often that they kill their fathers;
Which makes unreasonable a modern plot
As close-knit as the Greeks'. We have to suffice
With wholeness in the motive, defection in act,
For do we not in the middle of the century
Throw our arms about, seeing no mark to hit?
There is a further nicety. The Greeks
Had sense to keep the corpses off the stage,
It was not delicate, harmonious, or just.
Would you see the old man sputtering his life out,
A bloody lump, the lion Son slavering over him?

JASON

You've got the Oedipus complex here, or half
Of it; if not quite actual, half along.

ROBIN

The other half I think we'll not touch on.
It seems to read too much like literature.
I could not show him sleeping with his mother.
Even in snide report it would be laughable.

WENDY

A Comedy is supposed to make us laugh, is it not?

ROBIN

Wendy, you have not sifted definitions.
Laughter is incidental, may not occur at all.
The point's to show the folly of the world.

JASON

It's laughable enough to see men happy.
Make it light and gay. And keep worms away.
The subtlety is thus far thoroughly modern.
Robin has thought about his Oedipus,
Admired the precision of the plot, its flawlessness,

And gives the sense of our own inadequacy
In cambering part of it, in canting it off;
The partial view, the frustrate jibes, the energy.

BERYL

Let us get on. I'm afraid it is getting late.

ROBIN

We will change our serious plans, and make it short.
It is two years later now, on the Fourth of July.

Inner Scene VI

(*The office of the Professional Psychiatrist. Two years later.
The Fourth of July. Father and Mother*)

MOTHER

Good-day. I'm sorry we had to trouble you
And call you in today. It is important!

FATHER

This is the worst blow to my pride of all.

PROFESSIONAL PSYCHIATRIST

What has happened now?

FATHER

                                        Our son is married!

MOTHER

And to someone we do not know at all.
A telegram came last night from California.

FATHER

What is worse, he says he has become a Vedantist.

MOTHER

I now rather enjoy the marriage part,
After the first shock, and hope he will be happy.
But to marry someone we do not even know!
Maybe it is best. We have passed our service,
And must resign to blows; we came for sympathy.

FATHER

What a joke, to become a Vedantist on us.
I guess we shouldn't have come, to bother you.
I thought maybe you could do something about it.
But there is nothing to do, now, nothing to do.

PROFESSIONAL PSYCHIATRIST

No. There is nothing now to do about it.
He is of age, at present of sound mind,
At will to find his women and his foible.
Don't forget that life is a Comedy

> In which the players are neither pure nor free,
> But driven by will, and caught by destiny.
> Go home, and don't think about it too seriously.

FATHER

Good-bye, then.

MOTHER

Good-bye, Doctor.

PROFESSIONAL PSYCHIATRIST

Good-bye, good-bye.
(Shrugs his shoulders)
I wish I could find a case really interesting.
Men are rats treading in a confined cage,
All their steps are waltzes to the moon,
Escape they will not till the stop of doom,
Around we go, fast or slow, around.
(Exit)

ROBIN

The next scene is two years later, in the drawing room of the
parents, another Fourth of July.

Inner Scene VII

*(Two years later, during the war. Father and Mother in their
drawing room. Another fourth of July)*

MOTHER

I feel now that we are terribly to blame.

FATHER

I do not think that at all; I have not changed.

MOTHER

I cannot get rid of the feeling of shame.

FATHER

He has disgraced the family name.
Who would believe that I would have a son in prison?

MOTHER

It is all part of the same inexorable pattern.

FATHER

What can I tell my fellow officers in the Navy,
What can I tell them at the Puritan Club,
That I have a son who is a Pacifist in prison—
A conscientious objector for my only son.

MOTHER

There is nothing we can do about it.
It is all part of the same inexorable pattern.

Evil is smirking in the heart of all of us.
What a chance you take when you get married.
We should at least call the Doctor.

FATHER

I suppose so.

You call him.
(Mother goes to the telephone)

MOTHER

Hello, is it you, Doctor?
Yes, we are at home. Yes, we are all right.
We thought you would just want to hear our recent news.
Our son has become a conscientious objector.
Moreover, although we do not have the details,
He is lodged in the federal penitentiary
Where they have sentenced him to serve four years.
What, what did you say? Well, good-bye, good-night.
(To Father)
He said he hoped he would write great music there.

FATHER

He was the music of my early years.

MOTHER

I was the disharmony that had no tears.
Now that I am old, now that I am old, I have tears.
What a way to spend our Fourth of July.
(The players exit and come back into the front room)

ROBIN

That is the end of our first erogenous effort.

BERYL

Would anybody like another drink?

GRAYCE

I could use some more beer, if you have some.
(Others hold up whiskey glasses)

WENDY

Make mine light, please.

CHARLIE

Thanks, I would like one.

Beryl, it is artful and good. You ought to be pleased.

BERYL

Oh think of the time and the destraction fit.

JASON

Congratulations, Robin. A webbed, persuasive gain;
Quite subtle in spots, perhaps too long-winded.

GRAYCE
>Robin, I got the biggest kick out of it.

ROBIN
>You are all too kind. I am afraid it crepitates.
>Beryl, give the real actors something liquid.
>*(She goes out, comes back, fixing them)*

CHARLIE
>Only a certain tedium in soliloquy
>Seemed to keep it from moving fair and free.

JASON
>Why did you want to savor him as a Vedantist?
>I should have thought it a cult somewhat freak.
>I have known some who convinced themselves of it
>By way of getting out of going to war,
>Or so it would seem; none to espouse that ice
>After the harsh reality of their prison scenes.
>To throw in a marriage on top of it seems a bit thick.
>Is it logically probable? Do the notions cohere?
>Actually, do you know, are Vedantists allowed to marry?

ROBIN
>You may have me there. I will have to look it up.

WENDY
>Didn't you only want a touch of the bizarre?

JASON
>And to get in a somewhat unfashionable lick?
>It would be fashionable to have him turn Catholic.

ROBIN
>There is more than one way through a mazy way.
>You can skin a sheep from the eye or the lip.

BERYL
>I do not see anything wrong about the marriage.
>Who knows about life until he has tried it?
>It would be most natural, after being in prison.

GRAYCE
>Unless you wanted to make him a homosexual.

CHARLIE
>That would be tiresome, childish, and effete.

ROBIN
>And it would be much too conventional.
>Our brainy centers are replete with them.

JASON
>That would thin it to the one-dimensional
>Where we have it full-bodied, somewhat desperate.

ROBIN
> Do you have any more questions about it?
> I am afraid I still think it crepitates.

WENDY
> I'm afraid we must be going. It is getting late.

JASON
> What about the ending? Should it be dramatic?
> Can you let it peter out in intellection?

GRAYCE
> Come, Charlie, we have to be going too.

ROBIN
> Why not just let it fade into the quotidian?
> Leaving the theater we walk back into our own lives
> Which out-do in reality the stage's artifice.

JASON
> But maybe you are always too philosophic.

ROBIN
> All right, before our next meeting, I will invent
> Some robust, artful gesture to end it on.
> *(They all say good-bye and begin to depart. There is a loud
> knock at the door. Enter, Pendleton, the composer, flanked by
> two police officers. Pendleton addresses Robin angrily)*

PENDLETON
> You cannot get away with this. It is libelous.
> I heard that you were writing a play about me.
> I have come to stop it before it gets any further.
> This officer has a warrant for your arrest.

ROBIN *(Strenuously)*
> This is an invasion of my private rights.
> This is a private theater. We are guaranteed
> Freedom of speech, freedom, freedom of speech
> Under the Bill of Rights. The play is not about you.
> It is a play about the struggle of every man.
> It is a symbol of the struggle of any artist.
> If you like, we'll change it and make the protagonist
> A painter, a poet, or a dramatist. We mean no offense.

PENDLETON
> Officer, serve the warrant on this man.

ROBIN
> What sort of a society are we living in?
> We do not want a police state in America.

OFFICER
> Come along, tell it to the Judge.

ROBIN

> Can't you be reasonable? If I publish this work
> I'll print before it, "The characters in this play
> Are entirely fictitious and have no resemblance
> To any living person."

PENDLETON

> That would be a lie. Tell it in court.
> *(They take him out)*

(Curtain)

Notes

Notes About Previous Publication

Triptych appeared in *Burr Oaks* (Chatto and Windus, 1947, and Oxford University Press, 1947) and later in *Collected Poems, 1930-1960* (Chatto and Windus, 1960, and Oxford University Press, 1960).

Preamble I was published in *discovery* No. 6 (July, 1955).

Preamble II appeared in *The Sewanee Review* (Winter, 1954).

The Apparition was first published in *Poetry* (March, 1951).

The Visionary Farms appeared, in part, in *New World Writing* No. 3. An additional scene (Scene XV) was published in *Quarterly Review of Literature* (No. 3, 1955). Other additions have been made to earlier scenes.

Devils and Angels and *The Mad Musician* were first published in *The Tulane Drama Review* (Summer, 1962).

Denis Donoghue's The Third Voice: Modern British and American Verse Drama *(Princeton University Press, 1959) in Chapters 12 and 14 contains criticism and comment about* The Apparition *and* The Visionary Farms.

Notes About First Productions

The first production of The Poets' Theatre, Cambridge, Massachusetts, in January, 1951, included *The Apparition*, with the following cast:

Robin, the host	Donald Hall
Beryl, his wife	Renee Michaelson
Jason	Raymond Fitch
Wendy, his wife	Jean Liston
Charley	William Matchett
Grayce, his wife	Joan Rice
Girl	Kay Levy

Directed by Mrs. Mark DeWolf Howe

The first production of *The Visionary Farms* was by The Poets' Theatre, on May 21 and 23, 1952, at The Fogg Museum, Cambridge, Massachusetts, with the following cast:

Robin Everyman (Adam Fahnstock)	Robert A. Brooks
Beryl Everyman (Vine Fahnstock)	Frances Sternhagen
Jason Curley (Roger Parker)	Leonard Laster
Wendy Curley (Frieda Herzog)	Kay Levy
Charlie Westgate (Ruben Beanpole)	John Aubrey
Grayce Westgate	Sonia Grant
The Consulting Author	Russell H. Peck
Hurricane Ransome	Neil Powell
Peter Fahnstock (Bub Woodward)	Paul Priest
William Fahnstock (Jones Taft)	Johnson Montgomery
Suzanne Fahnstock	Eleanor Maclean
Jacob Herzog (Chief Decker)	Robert Boyajain
Salesman (Ted Parker)	Tom Kennedy

Directed by Jeanne Tufts and Frank Cassidy

The scenes were:

Scene I	Home of the Everymans
Scene II	Congregational Church
Scene III	Fahnstock's House
Scene IV	Office, The Visionary Farms

Scene V	The same, one month later
Scene VI	Ransome's Office
Scene VII	Fahnstock's Living Room, six months later
Scene VIII	Mr. Parker's Living Room
Scene IX	Barber Shop
Scene X	President's Office
Scene XI	Furniture Store
Scene XII	President's Office
Scene XIII	Apple Orchard
Scene XIV	Home of the Everymans

The first production of *The Mad Musician* was by The Poets'
Theatre, Cambridge, Massachusetts, in a concert reading on March
30 and 31 and April 1, 1962, with the following cast:

Charles Westgate, Schoolmaster	Fred Della Paolera
Joseph, Chorus I	Richard Simons
Beryl Everyman	Lilli Valun
Wendy Curley, Mother, Chorus II	Elizabeth McClymont
Grayce Westgate	Marie Claire Davis
Robin Everyman, Son, Chorus III	Theodore Jacobs
College psychiatrist, Arthur	Fred Bush
Father, Chorus II	Henry Dewing
Jason Curley, Professional psychiatrist	Hugh Leppo

Directed by Laurence Channing

The first production of *Devils and Angels* was by The Poets' Theatre,
Cambridge, Massachusetts, in a concert reading on March 30 and 31
and April 1, 1962, with the following cast:

Author	Fred Della Paolera
John, Professor II, Member of the audience, Mr. Masters	Jack Sheridan
Author's wife	Marie Claire Davis
Robin Everyman, Consulting author	Theodore Jacobs
Beryl Everyman, Robin's wife	Lilli Valun
Devil, Mr. Byfield	Richard Simons
Angel	Hugh Leppo
Professor I, Mr. Sly	Henry Dewing
Mrs. Sly, Sweetheart	Elizabeth McClymont

Directed by Robert Stewart

The Mad Musician *and* Devils and Angels *were also given reading
productions at the University of Pennsylvania, Philadelphia, on April 6,
1962, under the auspices of the Philomathean Society.*

The text of this book was composed in 10
point Kennerly, leaded one point, and the
Introduction in 12 point Kennerly, leaded
two points. The book was printed by letter-
press on 60 pound Warren's Olde Style,
wove finish, made by the S. D. Warren
Company. The book was manufactured by
The Seeman Printery, Incorporated, Durham,
North Carolina.